Simple Treatments for Complex Problems

A Patient Workbook

Simple Treatments for Complex Problems

A Patient Workbook

Kelly C. Cukrowicz
Andrea B. Burns
Jennifer A. Minnix
Lorraine R. Reitzel
Thomas E. Joiner Jr.

In collaboration with the staff of
The Florida State University Psychology Clinic

Leonardo Bobadilla
Jessica S. Brown
Melanie A. Butler
Kimberly A. Driscoll
Annya Hernandez
Donald R. Kerr Jr.
Rita L. Ketterman
Lindsey Kirsch
Elizabeth N. Lima
Justin D. Michels
Karla K. Repper
J. Anthony Richey
Sheila L. Stanley
Foluso M. Williams
LaRicka R. Wingate

Routledge
Taylor & Francis Group
LONDON AND NEW YORK

First published 2004 by Lawrence Erlbaum Associates, Inc.

Published 2021 by Routledge
2 Park Square, Milton Park, Abingdon, Oxon OX14 4RN
605 Third Avenue, New York, NY 10017

Routledge is an imprint of the Taylor & Francis Group, an informa business

Cover design by Kathryn Houghtaling Lacey

Library of Congress Cataloging-in-Publication Data

Simple treatments for complex problems. A patient workbook / Kelly C. Cukrowicz . . . [et al.] in collaboration with the staff of the Florida State University Psychology Clinic.
p. cm.
Includes bibliographical references and index.
ISBN 0-8058-4947-5 (pbk. : alk. paper)
1. Cognitive therapy—Problems, exercises, etc. I. Cukrowicz, Kelly C. II. Florida State University. Psychology Clinic.

RC489.C63S567 2004
16.89'142—dc26 2004050676
CIP

ISBN 13: 978-0-8058-4947-9 (pbk)

Contents

Acknowledgments

This workbook was a product of the collaborative efforts of the graduate student therapists of Florida State University Psychology Clinic and its director Thomas E. Joiner, Jr., PhD. Following completion of the main text, the students were enthusiastic about the potential for a workbook to illustrate the principles of SA for patients. The students are extremely grateful for Dr. Joiner's mentorship and generosity in fostering the completion of this workbook. We hope it will help patients to master widely used techniques that will help them move quickly along their road to recovery.

—Kelly C. Cukrowicz

Chapter 1

Introduction*

Your life span is made up of many interpersonal situations (brief interactions with others). How you feel and how you think about yourself and your life depends in large measure on how effectively you manage these situations. Do situations tend to come out the way you intended them to? Do you obtain the outcomes you desire? Unfortunately, many people do not get what they want (i.e., their desired outcome) in their interpersonal interactions and feel powerless to do anything about it. For some people, repeated failures to achieve desired outcomes can lead to feelings of frustration, negativity, pessimism, helplessness, depression, and/or anxiety. If you have experienced these emotions as a result of problems in interactions with others, this workbook is for you. It will teach you how to analyze interpersonal situations in your life in a way that will increase your chances of getting what you want out of them. Achieving desired outcomes more often will result in enhanced feelings of satisfaction with your relationships and improved emotional well-being overall.

The goal of this workbook is to help you develop a skill that will improve your life—perhaps even dramatically. This skill is called *Situational Analysis* (SA). SA is a new way of thinking about the interpersonal situations in your life. SA requires you to focus on your goals (i.e., desired outcomes) and teaches you to modify your thoughts and behaviors in order to achieve those goals. Why should you be convinced that SA will change

*The primary authors contributing to this chapter were Kelly C. Cukrowicz, Jennifer A. Minnix, Donald R. Kerr Jr., and Thomas E. Joiner Jr.

your life? SA has been demonstrated by its developers to relieve chronic depression (McCullough, 2000) and has been effective in treating a wide variety of psychological complaints, such as generalized anxiety, anger control problems, and discomfort in social situations, and interpersonal issues, such as parent–child interaction problems and partner relationship problems (Driscoll, Cukrowicz, Reardon, & Joiner, 2004).

Like any skill, SA requires some teaching and some practice to learn. This workbook will do at least part of the teaching, and you will do the practicing. SA may be most effective when learned in the context of therapy because, as with any higher level skill, learning from a professional can really facilitate the process. Consider tennis, for example. Although you can learn how to play tennis on your own, having an experienced pro to guide you, offer helpful feedback, and keep you motivated to practice regularly can help you to see results faster than if you were learning to play and practicing on your own. Similarly, learning SA can be enhanced by feedback from a therapist, and you may see results faster if you have help from an objective and practiced professional. However, if you are not currently seeing a therapist, do not despair. SA is a skill that you can also utilize effectively on your own if you work and practice hard.

In brief, SA is a sequence of steps you take to analyze interactions with another person. You can also use it to analyze interactions that occur "within" yourself, but at first it may be easier to see how SA works by focusing on interactions with others. As you will see, the steps are simple; however, they are not always easy. Each is described in detail in later chapters of this workbook, but the following will give you an idea of how it works. After choosing a brief interaction, you get out paper and pencil and proceed through the following steps:

1. Describe the essentials of what happened.
2. List your thoughts about or interpretations of what happened.
3. Describe how you behaved in the situation.
4. Describe how you wanted the situation to turn out.
5. Describe how the situation did turn out.
6. Did you get what you wanted?

If the answer to the last question is "yes," then celebrate. If the answer is "no," then you review your interpretations and behaviors as follows: For each interpretation and behavior, ask yourself whether it helped you to get what you wanted. If it did not, then come up with an interpretation or behavior that would have been more likely to help you get what you wanted.

Sound simple? Well, it can be, when you have done it for awhile and know what you are doing, but there are a number of problems and obstacles that can crop up along the way when you are first learning to use SA. The remaining chapters in this workbook describe, in great detail, each of the previously indicated steps and focus on teaching you how to do SA correctly. These chapters also explain the obstacles that people commonly encounter when first learning to use SA, so that you may avoid these pitfalls in your own practice of the technique. In addition, helpful worksheets are included, and case examples are described to enhance your understanding of how SA works and how SA can be applied to a number of different situations.

THE STEPS OF SITUATIONAL ANALYSIS

The following is a brief outline of the steps of SA. This is designed to give you an idea of what is to come in the chapters ahead. As you read this section, it might be helpful for you to think of an interpersonal situation in your life that did not turn out so well. How would this situation fit into the steps outlined below? Note how analyzing your situation in this way might be different than how you thought about it as it was happening. Even if it is quite different, do not worry—most of us do not think of our interpersonal situations as a series of "steps," and the whole process is likely to seem quite foreign at first. However, by the time you are finished reading this workbook, you will understand why using the steps of SA will help you to improve your interactions with others and help you achieve more satisfaction with the way those interactions turn out.

Step 1

Step 1 is to identify a *specific* situation in your life that was somewhat upsetting or stressful. In Step 1 you succinctly describe that problematic or stressful situation in an objective manner. This means that you describe the situation in a way that someone watching it happen would—in other words, as if you were a "fly on the wall." The goal during this step is for you to describe the highlights of the situation, including the beginning, middle, and end, without editorializing or making interpretations about what happened. See chapter 2 for a more detailed description of Step 1.

Steps 2 and 3

In Steps 2 and 3, you target your thoughts and behaviors regarding the situation identified in Step 1. During Step 2, you learn to identify the specific interpretations you made during the situation. In this case, an *interpretation* means either your thoughts during the situation or a description of what the situation meant to you. The goal of the second step is for you to determine what your interpretations were in the situation. Most people find that their interpretations tend to be global (not specific to the situation) and sometimes negative in nature. For example, some people might make an interpretation such as "he *always* makes me feel badly about myself" or "I *never* can do anything right." It is not hard to see why these examples would be considered both global and negative. However, as this workbook will teach you, the most effective interpretations are those that are specific to the situation at hand, focused on what you wanted to get in the situation, and directed toward how to proceed in getting what you want—that is, interpretations that will help you get what you want from a situation by, for example, leading you to action that is consistent with your desired outcome. Step 2 is described in detail in chapter 3.

During the third step of SA you identify the specific behaviors that occurred during the situation. Particular attention is paid to what was said, your tone of voice, body language, eye contact, and anything else that you did (e.g., walking away). As in Step 2, the goal of Step 3 is for you to focus on the aspects of your behavior that contribute to getting what you want. See chapter 4 for additional information about Step 3.

Steps 4 and 5

Steps 4 and 5 focus on *outcomes*. At Step 4 you consider what outcome you *wanted* or *desired* for the situation you described in Step 1. In other words, you determine how you would have preferred for things to turn out. This is called the *desired outcome* (DO). Your goal in Step 4 is to construct DOs that are attainable and realistic; meaning that the outcome is possible and that you have the capacity, or control, to produce the outcome. People often have difficulty determining the appropriate DO because they begin by choosing an outcome that requires change in another person. This type of DO may not be attainable, because you do not have control over someone else's behavior or desire to change. You must always focus on how *your* thoughts and behaviors influence situations. Also, it is important for you to identify only a single DO for each situation you describe in SA.

In Step 5 you consider how the situation described in Step 1 *actually* came out. This is called the *actual outcome* (AO). Your goal in Step 5 is to construct an AO using behavioral terminology. You will read more about what this means in chapter 5, but basically it refers to reporting what actually happened in the situation by stating the objective facts in a clear and succinct way. See Fig. 1.1 for an example of a blank SA worksheet containing all of the steps just described.

Summary of Steps 1–5

The philosophy of SA can be summarized as follows: If your DO (Step 4) and AO (Step 5) are discrepant, then something is wrong. When something is wrong, you need to look back to your thoughts (Step 2), behaviors (Step 3), or DO (Step 4) to determine where the problem lies. A common reason why Steps 4 and 5 are discrepant is that there is abandonment of personal control somewhere in the process. For example, you might be abandoning personal control if you think you did not get what you wanted because *someone else caused* you to make a mistake (an example of an interpretation in Step 2). Throughout the steps of SA, it is better to focus on something over which you can actually have control, namely, your own thinking and behavior. But how can you change them? The answer is to change them in a way that reduces the discrepancies between your AOs and DOs in specific, discrete situations (see Fig. 1.2).

Remediation Phase

When a DO is not achieved in a specific, discrete situation, SA recommends that you go back to your thoughts and behaviors and see how each hurt you or helped you in terms of getting your DO. This is called the *remediation phase.* Remediation might also be called the *change* phase. If a thought or behavior helped you—terrific, keep doing that, and try to do it even more in the future. But if a thought or behavior hurt you—got in the way of your getting your DO—you need to try something different and evaluate whether the different thought or behavior might have produced a more desirable outcome.

In the remediation phase, your behaviors and thoughts are targeted for change and revised so that your new behaviors and thoughts in the situation better contribute to the DO. So, when you go back through Step 2,

Situational Analysis

Name: ____

Date of Situational Event: ______________________________

Situational Area: ______ Family ______ Work/School ______ Social

Select a stressful situation that has occurred in your life during the previous week or two. Please describe this situation using the steps indicated below.

1. In three or four sentences, describe the situation.

2. What was your interpretation of the situation? What did this situation mean to you?
   a.
   b.
   c.
   d.

3. What were your behaviors in this situation?
   a. Eye Contact—
   b. Body Posture—
   c. Gestures—
   d. Tone of Voice—
   e. Timing—
   f. Other behaviors—

   What did you say? How did you say it?

4. State what you wanted to get out of this situation. What was your desired outcome?

5. What was the actual outcome of this situation?

RATE: Did you get what you wanted? Yes _______ No _______

FIG. 1.1. Situational analysis. Figure adapted from McCullough (2000) by Maureen Lyons Reardon.

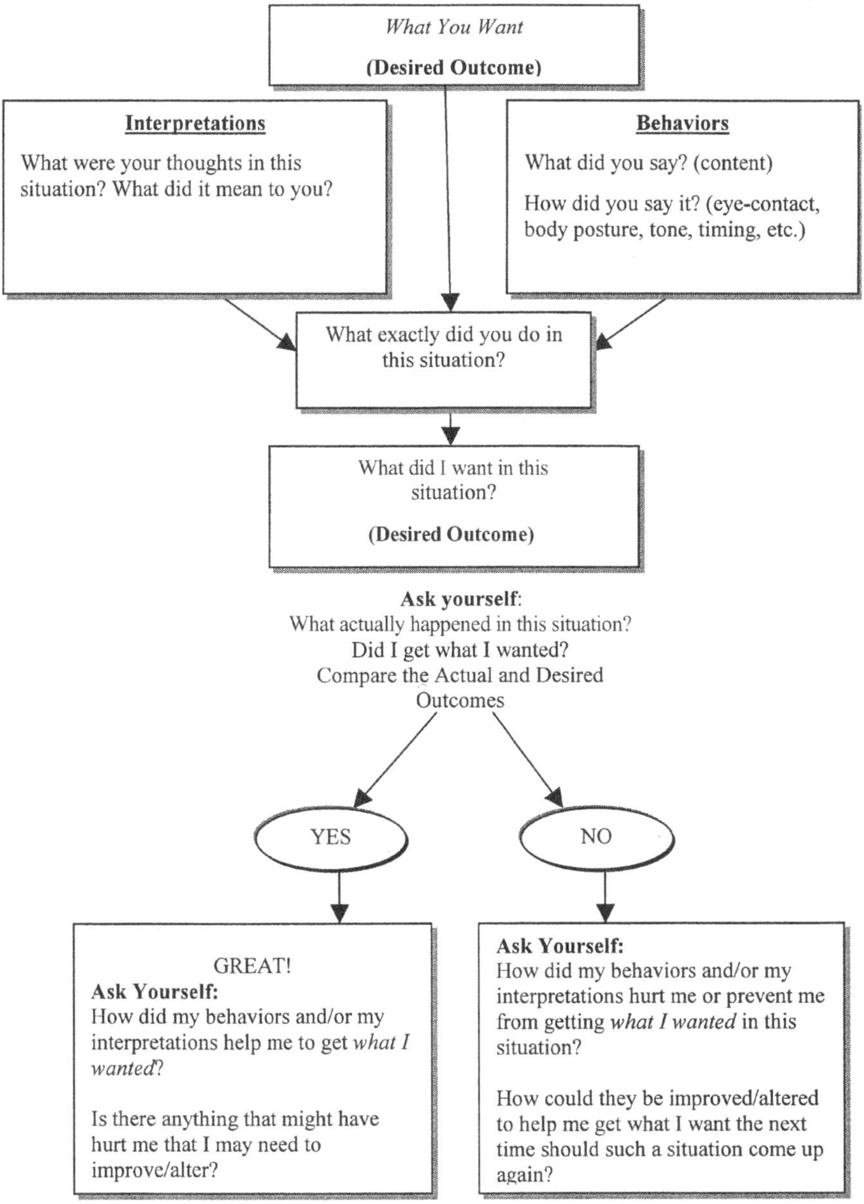

FIG. 1.2. Graphical depiction of the steps of situational analysis. Note the connections among thoughts, behaviors, and resulting outcomes. Figure created by Maureen Lyons Reardon.

each interpretation or thought is examined as to whether the interpretation aided or hindered you in the attainment of the DO. If it hindered your achievement of the DO, then you change it so that it becomes more helpful to that end. Changing behaviors in Step 3 is similar to that which is done when going back through Step 2. Each behavior is evaluated as to whether the behavior aided in the attainment of the DO or whether it hindered the attainment of the DO. If it hindered your achieving the DO, you change it so that it becomes more helpful to that end. SA is simply the repetition of these steps, situation after situation.

Once you have learned these steps of SA, you will be able to better analyze how you manage situations in your life. At first, you will be examining situations that have already happened. Of course, you cannot go back in time and "redo" these situations; however, once you have practiced SA, you may start to realize that there are patterns across situations in your thoughts, behaviors, and DOs that have not been working for you. When you start to recognize these patterns, you can begin to practice SA *while the situation is occurring.* That means you will start changing your "automatic" and hurtful thoughts and behaviors to those that are more helpful—thoughts and behaviors that you had previously been generating during the remediation phase of SA—right when the situation is happening. Over time, this will result in your getting better outcomes, having more satisfying relationships, and feeling better about yourself and your life.

HOW CAN SITUATIONAL ANALYSIS HELP YOU?

SA is helpful for a variety of reasons. First, the initial step of SA requires you to think about a *specific* stressful situation. This situation should be relatively short in duration. Much benefit can be gained from thinking of life as a series of small encounters. It is easier to control and to imagine DOs for small encounters. On the other hand, when you think of your life as a whole, many of life's problems, such as marital difficulties, depression, or anxiety, can seem so huge that it is overwhelming to imagine how to begin to change them. There are just too many details and too many situations to manage. Consider the example of a couple with marital problems. The couple originally states that they do not communicate effectively. This is a pretty global problem and not at all tied to a specific situation. It seems a rather daunting thing to try to fix. In contrast, imagine if they said they did not communicate effectively during one specific situation. This is more manageable, because they can influence *one* situation, whereas they are less likely to be effective in changing a global problem. It is important to remember that progress regarding specific situations is likely to generalize to other situations, much like a small pebble thrown into a pond sends ripples throughout the whole pond.

A second way in which SA is therapeutic is in learning to identify what you want in specific situations. In SA, this means learning to label DOs. Why is this important? Labeling DOs is important because it is hard to get what you want if you do not stop to decide what that is. In addition, determining what you want will help you begin to understand what is getting in your way when you do not get what you want. Finally, once you know what you want, you can start to communicate this to important people in your life.

Finally, SA is helpful because it teaches you how to get what you want out of situations. Specifically, it teaches you how to examine what you think and what you do to see if these thoughts and/or actions are getting in your way. Once you learn that you are doing or thinking specific things that aren't helpful in attaining what you want, you can begin changing them. By doing so, you will have taken control of your life, one situation at a time, and you will be getting what you want through your own actions.

CASE EXAMPLE: ANDY AND BETH

Because the steps of SA may be difficult for you at the beginning, a case example will be used to show you how SA works. This case example concerns a client in therapy, Andy, who was experiencing communication difficulty with his fiancée. In this chapter we introduce you to Andy's situation and his associated thoughts and behaviors. In each subsequent chapter, you will see how Andy analyzed his own contribution to the negative situation and what steps he took to achieve his own DO. As you read about each step, you can follow Andy's example to get an idea of how this process can be helpful to individuals with difficult situations to overcome. By the end of the workbook, you will be able to clearly see how each step in the SA process can be mastered and used to increase positive outcomes in your own life.

Background

Andy is a 24-year-old man who came to therapy seeking guidance in dealing with his relationship with his fiancée, Beth. Andy and Beth had been dating for two years and became engaged three months prior to the onset of Andy's therapy. Andy reported that while he and Beth were dating, they spent most of their time together and seldom fought. They worked in the same building, exercised at the same gym, and often stayed overnight at his apartment. He introduced her to his friends, and they rarely spent any time away from one another. After they had dated for a year, Andy began discussing long-term relationship plans with Beth. After another year, she agreed to marry him. Andy knew that she felt pressure from him, their friends, and her family to marry him, but he was convinced that he and Beth would live happily ever after. Unfortunately, Beth seemed less optimistic about their future. She seemed more stressed about planning their wedding than excited. Andy reported that he was very supportive of Beth and went out of his way to do things for her. He even paid off the massive amount of credit card debt that she acquired before they began dating and helped her with her rent from time to time. Beth often marveled about "how nice" he was. Andy described their relationship before the engagement as "perfect, each of our personalities complements the other—she is the opinionated one, and I'm the easygoing one." He reported that she seemed very happy in the relationship at that time and was very loving and affectionate toward him. He attributed Beth's ambivalence about the marriage to her past relationships with men, which had been emotionally painful and verbally abusive.

At the time of the engagement, Andy and Beth decided to move in together. Since they had been living with one another, Andy reported that they seemed to spend less time together than they used to. He felt distanced from her and insecure about their relationship. Andy reported that they argued often but never seemed to resolve the problems in the relationship. He felt that Beth was pulling away from him, spending more time with her friends, and going out on the weekends without him. When they were together, Andy felt that they seldom talked or interacted in a meaningful way. Andy described feeling frustrated, sad, and nervous that the relationship would continue to deteriorate. He felt that Beth was the dominant person in the relationship and that she seemed to be "looking for a fight" much of the time. He described himself as accommodating and easygoing. He felt that he was an easy person to get along with and did not understand Beth's constant agitation with him. In turn, he felt that she did not understand his feelings of rejection and loneliness. However, he reported that he seldom confronted her directly because he did not want to start a fight if it could be avoided. Andy's goals in therapy were to learn to communicate more productively with Beth and find a way to mend their relationship.

Andy was beginning to doubt that Beth truly loved him. She seemed annoyed with him constantly, even though he felt as if he was the same person he had always been. She was not affectionate toward him, and eventually told him that she often did not feel sexually attracted to him. She avoided hugging and kissing him, and often slept on the couch, claiming that she just "fell asleep watching television." He was unable to talk to her productively about the problems in their relationship. She seemed very depressed and began treatment with a therapist. She refused to discuss her feelings of sadness with him and seemed to express emotion only when she was angry. She got angry at him for simple things at times, such as refusing to decide what restaurant to go to for dinner or what to watch on television. Andy felt that most of the time Beth was either aggravated with him or just quiet and unresponsive. She also expressed often feeling guilty about hurting Andy, although her feelings of agitation remained. She wanted Andy to express his opinions and not be afraid to confront her. She felt as if he should be angry with her at times, but when he showed no emotion except sadness, she felt guilty and angry with him. She wanted him to understand that she needed time to herself every once in awhile. She hated when he sulked if she went out with her friends, because she always ended up feeling guilty for leaving him and was unable to relax and enjoy herself. Beth felt overwhelmed with pressure and emptiness. She wanted to feel love for Andy as she did before the engagement. Most of her friends told her that her fears about the wedding were just "cold feet" that would not last. However, she felt helpless to change her situation and trapped in a relationship in which she was no longer happy.

Example Situation

Next is an example of a difficult, but specific interpersonal event that occurred between Andy and Beth. This situation is ideal for SA because it was a situation in which there was a large gap between Andy's goal, or DO, and the AO of the event. Andy chose to complete an SA worksheet on this predicament and bring it in to discuss with his therapist. Andy's original SA worksheet is presented in Fig. 1.3.

Andy's Situation

Beth went out again with her friends on Friday night. They were going to a club to dance and drink. She did not invite me to join them but rather passively suggested that I hook up with some of my friends for a "boys'

Situational Analysis Worksheet

Name: *Andy*

Date of Situational Event: *March 4, 2004*

Situational Area: ________ Family ________ Work/School ________ Social

Instructions: Select a stressful situation that has occurred in your life during the previous week. Please describe the situation using the steps indicated below.

1. Describe what happened:

   Beth went out again with her friends on Friday night. They were going to a club to dance and drink. She did not invite me to join them, but rather, passively suggested that I hook up with some of my friends for a "boys' night out." I told her to have a good time. She got all dressed up, kissed me on the cheek, and left. I stayed home and watched TV. She got home at 2:30 in the morning, happy and tired. She didn't even ask me how my night went.

2. Describe your interpretation(s) of what happened:

   1. *Beth should have known that I would want her to invite me along.*
   2. *I'm not going to tell her that I'm upset because she'll just get angry.*
   3. *She'd rather hang out with her friends than me, like she doesn't even like me any more.*
   4. *She doesn't even care that I spent the whole night by myself—again.*

3. Describe what you did during the situation:

   1. *All I said was for her to have fun. I didn't ask if I could come along.*
   2. *Tone of voice: "defeated". I didn't sound happy when she left.*
   3. *I wouldn't look at her or smile. I just ignored her and watched TV.*
   4. *When she came home, I was very quiet and didn't respond when she told me how much fun she'd had.*

4. Describe how you wanted the event to come out for you (Desired Outcome):

   I wanted her to want me to come along. I wanted her to realize that she's being rude by leaving me out and making me feel rejected.

5. Describe how the event came out for you (Actual Outcome):

   We got into an argument when she got home. She told me I made her feel guilty by "pouting" and said that she just needed some space to be on her own. I just let it go and went to sleep on the couch, but I felt awful. She just seemed agitated with me.

RATE: Did you get what you wanted? Yes _____ No *X*

FIG. 1.3. Andy's situational analysis worksheet. Figure adapted from McCullough (2000) by Jennifer A. Minnix.

night out." I told her to have a good time. She got all dressed up, kissed me on the cheek, and left. I stayed home and watched TV. She got home at 2:30 in the morning, happy and tired. She didn't even ask me how my night went.

Andy's Interpretations

1. Beth should have known that I would want her to invite me along.
2. I'm not going to tell her that I'm upset because she will just get angry.
3. She'd rather hang out with her friends than me, like she doesn't even like me anymore.
4. She doesn't even care that I spent the whole night by myself—again.

Andy's Behaviors

1. All I said was for her to have fun. I didn't ask her if I could come along.
2. My tone of voice was "defeated"—I didn't sound happy with her when she left. I wouldn't look at her or smile—I just sort of ignored her and watched TV.
3. When she came home, I was very quiet and didn't really respond when she told me how much fun she had had.

Desired Outcome

I wanted her to want me to come along. I wanted her to realize that she's being rude by leaving me out and making me feel rejected.

Actual Outcome

We got into an argument when she got home. She told me I make her feel guilty by "pouting" and said that she just needed some space to be on her own. I just let it go and went to sleep on the couch, but I felt awful. She just seemed agitated with me.

SUMMARY AND CONCLUSIONS

The purpose of this workbook is to provide you with a practical foundation for implementing SA for a variety of life problems. Simply put, SA is a strategy that can help anyone to get what he or she wants out of situations in his or her life. In the chapters that follow, each step of SA is described in detail. Common problems of each step are discussed, and case examples (Andy's case plus additional examples) and helpful worksheets are provided to enhance your understanding of the material and illustrate the utility of SA in your life. The modification and adaptation of SA is described in a straightforward fashion so that individuals who lack formal training in its implementation can easily use it with or without a therapist's assistance. This technique is fairly easy to learn and will provide rewards for anyone who learns it! So, get ready to learn the steps of SA and start getting what you want from situations in your life!

Chapter 2

Step 1: Situational Description*

Do you ever catch yourself saying things like "bad things always happen to me," "nobody likes me," or "I am not good enough"? If so, you are not alone. Many people tend to think about their problems in very general terms like these. It is interesting, though, that our lives—including our problems—are made up of numerous discrete situations, such as phone conversations, work meetings, and shopping trips. In the first step of Situational Analysis (SA) you work on changing this global way of thinking and learn how to focus on specific situations. This exercise is helpful because it takes your attention away from your general (and sometimes overwhelming) feelings and thoughts about your problems and focuses your attention instead on one particular instance in which you experienced the problem. As the other chapters of this workbook will show, by conducting many SAs and looking at many specific situations like these you will find general patterns that are common in your interactions with others. In other words, you can learn to tackle your big, general problems one little situation at a time.

WHAT HAPPENS AT STEP 1?

The goal of the first step of SA is to be able to briefly and accurately describe a distressing or stressful situation. The first thing you need to do is

*The primary authors contributing to this chapter were LaRicka R. Wingate, Elizabeth N. Lima, and Melanie A. Butler.

to think of a situation that was particularly distressing for you. Often these situations include an interaction with another person. For example, you could think about the last argument that you had with your spouse, a time that your boss upset you, or an upsetting phone call that you had with your best friend. Any situation will work, as long as it was meaningful to you. It's generally best to focus on situations that you found to be particularly distressing first; however, less distressing situations will work as well. As long as the situation was somewhat upsetting, sad, worrisome, difficult, stressful, or painful to you, analyzing it with SA will be helpful.

Once you have picked a situation that was distressing, you then need to narrow that situation down even further, to highlight the most important, most significant part of that situation. It is often helpful to think of your task as selecting a particular *slice of time*. For instance, an appropriate slice of time for SA could involve an interaction that lasted up to 15 minutes or so. What is most important is to get to the heart of the main interaction, or the part that was most bothersome to you. For example, if you are focusing on the last argument you had with your spouse, the description of the situation should include only one specific time spent arguing. Do not include what you were doing before the argument, what you or the other person were thinking, or what you did after the argument—just focus on the slice of time during which the argument occurred. Even if the argument was ongoing, taking place over the course of several days, or weeks, or even longer, it will be critical for SA that you choose one *specific* instance in which you and your spouse were arguing and focus for the moment only on that.

Most people would agree that every good story has a beginning, a middle, and an end point, and it is important that the description of your slice of time have these elements as well. A clear beginning point indicates that an interaction has begun, or, more specifically, what started the interaction. For example, the beginning point of a situation could be when someone made a statement to you, when the phone rang, or when you opened the door. Next, the situation should have a middle. This is the meat of what happened, or the main goings-on during the situation. Last, the situation needs a clear ending point. This indicates that the particular interaction you selected for analysis had ended. For example, the ending point of the situation could be when you slammed the door or hung up the phone. To be complete, your description of the situation should have a clear beginning, middle, and ending.

When describing the situation at Step 1, be careful not to editorialize it. This means that you must not include your thoughts, feelings, or opinions about the situation. If the situation includes phrases like "I thought she would be so mad," or "He must have thought I was an idiot," you are editorializing. Remember, your job at this step is to describe just the facts, or what someone else would see if they were watching you. Try to describe the situation as if it were a silent movie, or imagine what a fly on the wall would have seen. Following these basic guidelines will help you generate a situational description that has a beginning, middle, and end and includes only the facts.

WHY FOCUS ON STEP 1?

It is extremely difficult to problem-solve when you try to take on several different problems at one time. That is why, as simple as it sounds, it's important to for you to take a "just the facts, ma'am" perspective and stick to describing only what happened in *one* particular situation. At first, this task may prove to be more difficult than it sounds, because it is natural to speak in more global terms and editorialize, or include your opinion about situations. When people experience a particularly distressing situation, it is common to think "everything is going wrong," or "I can't do anything right." The problem is that such general and abstract statements or thoughts have a tendency to increase feelings of helplessness and hopelessness about the future and to make it difficult to implement positive changes. Furthermore, worrying about global circumstances can leave you feeling so overwhelmed that you don't even know where to begin attempts to solve them—in fact, solving them at all may seem impossible! This is exactly why the first step of SA requires you to describe a *specific* event that involves a significant interaction with another person. If you approach your problem at this specific level instead of a general one, your problem will seem much less overwhelming and therefore much easier to fix.

This first step of SA not only is useful in its own right but also is invaluable for the effectiveness of the rest of the SA approach to problem solving. Creating a tight, clearly defined framework for a specific, meaningful event allows for a much more precise analysis of your thoughts and behaviors during that event, and for your personal goals (desired outcomes [DOs]) for that event, than a general approach would allow. And as the next few chapters will show, it is only by identifying these thoughts and behaviors that you can effect real change. Step 1 therefore provides the framework for the remaining steps of the treatment process. Learning to describe meaningful situations in concise, direct terms increases the likelihood that you will identify relevant and accurate interpretations, behaviors, actual outcomes (AOs), and DOs in the remaining steps. The more concise your initial description is, the more accessible your interpretations and behaviors will be.

In general, you will see that the way that you think and behave in a particular situation or slice of time that you select for SA has implications for how you think and behave at other times, in other situations. As this chapter has emphasized, to focus on one specific situation at a time is far easier than trying to analyze your whole life at once, and the specific situations you choose to examine will highlight patterns that are common throughout your life. Your approach to interpersonal situations is not random but is characterized by consistent patterns of thoughts and behaviors. The structure and specificity provided in your description at Step 1 will naturally bring order to the other steps of SA and to your approach to problems in general. In essence, the ability to closely examine discrete time periods will at once help you to uncover your general patterns of behavior and will make problem solving more manageable. Noting the outcome of your thoughts and behaviors in past situations will help you to mindfully alter your thoughts and behaviors in future interactions. Accordingly, the skills you acquire through repeated close examination of specific, meaningful situations will increase the probability of obtaining your DOs in the future.

Although Step 1 may seem fairly difficult at first, with regular and consistent practice it will become second nature. Eventually you will easily be able to focus in on the facts of one particular situation at a time, and you will no longer feel overwhelmed as you do when you try to consider several interpersonal situations at once. Mastering this step, along with the steps described in the other chapters of this workbook, will teach you the skills you need to anchor your problems in time and space and, ultimately, to get your DOs.

ANDY AND BETH'S SITUATION

Now let's take a look at Andy's case as an example of the proper way to handle Step 1. Remember that the goal of Step 1 is to briefly and accurately describe a distressing situation. Step 1 of Andy's SA was originally written like this:

> Beth went out again with her friends on Friday night. They were going to a club to dance and drink. She did not invite me to join them, but rather, passively suggested that I hook up with some of my friends for a "boys' night out." I told her to have a good time. She got all dressed up, kissed me on the cheek, and left. I stayed home and watched TV. She got home at 2:30 in the morning, happy and tired. She didn't even ask me how my night went.

You may notice a couple of problems with this description, in light of the guidelines for this step discussed earlier in this chapter. Given that we should *stay focused on only one situation* and *specify a clear beginning, middle, and end point,* the following changes to Andy's description of the event will make his story consistent with the structure of Step 1.

First, this step requires a clear and specific slice of time, and the sentence "Beth went out *again* with her friends on Friday night" implies more than one situation. This description of the event has no clear beginning. Focusing on the specific interaction would sound more like "Beth told me that she was going to a club with her friends to dance and drink." This description delineates a specific beginning point and refers to only one situation.

Second, the end of Andy's interaction with Beth is marked by his reply to her: "I told her to have a good time." Consistent with the goals of Step 1, this sentence indicates a clear ending point to the situation. The last sentences, "She got all dressed up, kissed me on the cheek, and left. I stayed home and watched TV. She got home at 2:30 in the morning, happy and tired. She didn't even ask me how my night went," make references to other slices of time and, hence, other situations.

The interior sentence, "She did not invite me to join them, but rather, passively suggested that I hook up with some of my friends for a 'boys' night out,' " provides necessary details to make a coherent story (i.e., the middle). No changes are needed there.

The revisions to Andy's original situation produce a description of the event consistent with the goals of Step 1. Here is Step 1 with a focus on only one situation and enclosed within clear beginning and end points:

> Beth told me that she was going to a club with her friends to dance and drink. She did not invite me, but suggested that I hook up with some friends for a "boys' night out." I told her to have a good time.

Andy began with a situation description that was not ideal for SA, but after a couple of specific revisions, Andy's situational description is now succinct and describes one specific slice of time.

COMMON STUMBLING BLOCKS

Succinctly describing a distressing situation at Step 1 takes practice, and you may encounter some obstacles along the way. At times, you may find it difficult to focus on only one event when there are several distressing events going on in your life. Initially, it may be difficult for you to see the large-scale implications of examining how your thoughts and actions in one event can have an impact on the quality of your personal relationships in general. Remember, though, that those specific situations often mirror other situations and areas of your life, and you will soon be able to recognize how this approach can work for many of your concerns. It's important, therefore, that you remain patient when learning this step.

Another obstacle that people often encounter is the challenge of describing a slice of time without editorializing. You may find it difficult to stop guessing about what others are thinking or what their actions mean, or to interject your own read on the situation. Don't worry—these thoughts of yours do matter in the SA process. However, that will come at the next step. All that matters in Step 1 is learning to establish the basic facts of the situation so that you can set the stage for all the thoughts and behaviors that you'll be examining later.

OTHER EXAMPLES

In order for you to get a better understanding of how a situational description at Step 1 should be generated, several illustrative examples of situational descriptions and the appropriate revisions are provided next. For further practice, you can also try reviewing the sample situations on the worksheet provided (see Fig. 2.1). As you consider these descriptions, keep in mind the following necessary characteristics of Step 1 that were considered to make the needed changes:

1. Describe a specific slice of time.
2. Focus on only one situation.
3. Include a clear beginning and end point.
4. Have a story that is internally coherent (i.e., the middle).
5. Avoid editorializing the situation.

Worksheet for Step 1: Situational Descriptions

Evaluate the following situational descriptions:

1) "Women reject me all the time. No one will ever love me."

a) Does the description have a clear beginning point? Yes No
b) Does the description have a clear end point? Yes No
c) Does the description have a story that is internally coherent? Yes No
d) Does the description involve a discrete time period (slice of time)? Yes No
e) Is the description free of thoughts and feelings (editorializing)? Yes No
f) Briefly list the problem(s) with the situational description.

____

____

____

____

2) "Wednesday I went to apply for retirement benefits. I filled out all of the forms that they asked me to fill out. This has been going on forever and it is really wearing me down. After I filled out the forms, the employee there told me I could leave and she would get back with me. I got in my car and went home."

a) Does the description have a clear beginning point? Yes No
b) Does the description have a clear end point? Yes No
c) Does the description have a story that is internally coherent? Yes No
d) Does the description involve a discrete time period (slice of time)? Yes No
e) Is the description free of thoughts and feelings (editorializing)? Yes No
f) Briefly list the problem(s) with the situational description.

____

____

____

____

FIG. 2.1. *(Continued)*

Worksheet for Step 1: Situational Descriptions *(continued)*

3) "I called my mom on the phone yesterday. We were on the phone for about five minutes and I told her that I was hurt because she did not come to visit me last week. She apologized and then we hung up."

   a) Does the description have a clear beginning point? Yes No
   b) Does the description have a clear end point? Yes No
   c) Does the description have a story that is internally coherent? Yes No
   d) Does the description involve a discrete time period (slice of time)? Yes No
   e) Is the description free of thoughts and feelings (editorializing)? Yes No
   f) Briefly list the problem(s) with the situational description.

   ____

   ____

   ____

   ____

4) "When I got home from work last Monday I asked Jason if he had completed his homework. He said yes and continued playing his video game. I got a call from his teacher today, one week later, and she said Jason has not been completing his homework. I punished Jason by taking away his video game privileges."

   a) Does the description have a clear beginning point? Yes No
   b) Does the description have a clear end point? Yes No
   c) Does the description have a story that is internally coherent? Yes No
   d) Does the description involve a discrete time period (slice of time)? Yes No
   e) Is the description free of thoughts and feelings (editorializing)? Yes No
   f) Briefly list the problem(s) with the situational description.

   ____

   ____

   ____

   ____

FIG. 2.1. *(Continued)*

5) "My husband and I were watching the news last night. He wanted me to clean the house and do the dishes, but I didn't feel like it. He started talking really loud, calling me bad names, and saying how he wants to leave me. I started crying and begging him not to leave me. He just turned away, went to our bedroom, and shut the door."

   a) Does the description have a clear beginning point? Yes No

   b) Does the description have a clear end point? Yes No

   c) Does the description have a story that is internally coherent? Yes No

   d) Does the description involve a discrete time period (slice of time) Yes No

   e) Is the description free of thoughts and feelings (editorializing)? Yes No

   f) Briefly list the problem(s) with the situational description.

FIG. 2.1. Worksheet for Step 1: Situational descriptions. Figure created by LaRicka R. Wingate, Elizabeth N. Lima, and Melanie R. Butler.

Rosa's Situation

> My boss asked if I could help her out this weekend with a project. I wanted to tell her that my husband and I had made plans months in advance to leave town this weekend, but I started to think that she must really need my help. So, I told her that I could definitely come in to work over the weekend. I knew my husband was going to get mad, but I could not do otherwise. She then said thank you.

There are several instances where editorializing of the situation takes place. The sentences "I wanted to tell her that my husband and I had made plans months in advance, but I started to think that she must really need my help," and "I knew my husband was going to get mad, but I could not do otherwise," are references to what Rosa was thinking during the situation. These sentences fail to describe the situation in a "just the facts" or a "this happened, then this" format. Eliminating these sentences makes the situation similar to a silent movie, or to a fly on the wall perspective.

Revisions to Rosa's original situation produce a description of the event consistent with the goals of Step 1.

Rosa's Revised Situation

> My boss asked if I could help her out this weekend with a project. I told her that I could definitely come in to work over the weekend. She then said thank you.

Michael's Situation

> Sammy, my son, and I were at the supermarket. Before we went to the store I had told him that I was only buying the things on the list. As we were walking through the aisles, he kept saying "Daddy I want this, please get me that." I put one or two things he wanted in the cart. He kept asking for more. I told him, "We've already put things you wanted in the cart and I told you that we were only buying the items on the list, so no more." He kept insisting on getting more and more items and I kept telling him no. He started yelling and crying. I ended up getting the things he wanted.

Remember, this step requires that the focus be on only one situation. The sentence, "Before we went to the store I had told him that I was only buying the things on the list" refers to a situation that took place before the current interaction at the supermarket. Eliminating this sentence will make this situation fit into Step 1 of SA. The remaining sentences illustrate an event with a clear beginning and end point and thus a coherent story.

Michael's Revised Situation

> Sammy, my son, and I were at the supermarket. As we were walking through the aisles, he kept saying "Daddy I want this, please get me that." I put one or two things he wanted in the cart. He kept asking for more. I told him "no" several times, but he kept insisting. He started yelling and crying. I ended up getting the things he wanted.

Angela's Situation

> I came in from work and I found John on the couch drinking with bottles lying around everywhere. When I saw what was going on, I got upset and began yelling at him. I'm tired of his drinking, and all of that money going nowhere when we have so many bills to pay. The doctor has said that his health is no good. He doesn't do anything; all he does is drink and drink. He became defensive.

Deviations from what happened in the situation are evident in the following sentences: "I'm tired of his drinking, and all of that money going nowhere when we have so many bills to pay. The doctor has said his health is no good. He doesn't do anything; all he does is drink and drink." These sentences all include editorializing that is not part of the basic, factual description of the situation. Again, it's not that these kinds of statements are unimportant; rather, it's that they are not part of Step 1 (they are addressed in a later step).

In addition, a clear end point is lacking in the situation. The last sentence, "He became defensive," appears to indicate that an interaction between Angela and her husband took place. However, details on what happened next are not given.

Angela's Revised Situation

> I came in from work and I found John on the couch drinking with bottles lying around everywhere. When I saw what was going on, I got upset and began yelling at him. He became defensive. He told me to leave him alone. I kept saying that he has to stop drinking so much. He walked out of the living room and left the house.

Marcus's Situation

> I picked up my car from the shop yesterday. I ended up paying all the charges and stormed out of the shop pretty mad.

This story has a clear beginning and end point; however, it lacks an internally coherent story (i.e., the middle) that describes the interaction during the situation.

Marcus's Revised Situation

> I picked up my car from the shop yesterday. The cashier told me that there were more problems than anticipated and the charges came up to $300. I paid the charges and stormed out of the shop pretty mad.

Sarah's Situation

> I was at the bank trying to deposit Friday's paycheck. I already had a list in my mind of all the bills I needed to pay. After the teller checked my account, he let me know that my new balance was $158 because I had bounced several checks and that bank charges needed to be paid first. I thought, "Oh my God, what am I supposed to do now? How am I going to get through this month?" I almost started crying. I left the bank very worried about how I was going to pay all of my bills.

For this story to be congruent with the requirements of Step 1, several instances of editorializing need to be corrected. The following sentences are not consistent with the specifications necessary to properly describe the situation: "I already had a list in mind of all the bills I needed to pay . . . I thought, 'Oh my God, what am I supposed to do now? How am I going to get through this month?' " Eliminating these sentences makes the story fit the "this happened, then that" format.

Sarah's Revised Situation

> I was at the bank trying to deposit Friday's paycheck. After the teller checked my account, he let me know that my new balance was $158 because I had bounced several checks and that bank charges needed to be paid first. I almost started crying. I left the bank very worried about how I was going to pay all of my bills.

Ramon's Situation

> I got a speeding ticket when I was driving home yesterday. I'm still thinking about it. I don't know what I was thinking driving so fast.

Although the previous sentences provide some details about the event, the description lacks a clear end point and an internal coherent story. The reader is missing information regarding the interaction that took place during this situation, and it is not clear where or when the situation ends. Moreover, the last sentence contains some clear editorializing and thus should not be included in this step.

Ramon's Revised Situation

> I was driving on the highway, trying to rush home. A cop pulled me over and asked for my driver's license and registration. I tried to plead with the officer to just give me a warning, explaining to him that I typically do not speed but that I had serious circumstances. The officer gave me a ticket anyway.

SUMMARY AND CONCLUSIONS

By reading this chapter, you have learned the most important elements of the first step in SA. Specifically, you have learned to describe a specific slice of time with a clear beginning, middle, and end point. As you have seen, this is a particularly helpful step because it helps you to get away from those negative, global thoughts that can be overwhelming and to focus instead on a particular, more manageable situation. Step 1 is also important because, as the first step in SA, it helps guide your success in the remaining steps. Remember, truly mastering this step will take some practice and patience, but the payoff will be well worth the effort. Now that you have a good sense of the process at Step 1: Situational Description, you can confidently move on to Step 2: Situational Interpretations, and (finally!) take a look at those thoughts and opinions you've been forced to censor until now.

Chapter 3

Step 2: Interpretation of the Situation*

This chapter focuses on Step 2 of Situational Analysis (SA). You will learn why the second step is valuable (both within the context of SA and on its own), how to complete this step, and how to troubleshoot when presented with obstacles to completing it. Finally, you will be shown how Andy, our client who is experiencing strife in his relationship with his fiancée, navigates this step given the situation in which his fiancée spends the evening out with friends and Andy feels hurt.

You have already learned how to identify a situation to plug into SA (Step 1). You have been asked to describe the situation without giving information about how people in the situation thought or felt; in fact, you have been asked to focus on the *action* of the situation as though you were an observer rather than a participant. Step 2 requires that you dig deeper into your memory of the situation and bring back the most prominent thoughts you had in the situation. It can be difficult at first to tease apart the action of a situation and your thoughts or interpretations during it. When people recount situational stories, they naturally integrate what happened with how they perceived it. For example, think of the last time you told a friend a story about an exciting or frustrating situation you encountered. You probably infused the action of the story with your own

*The primary authors contributing to this chapter were Karla K. Repper, Andrea B. Burns, and Kimberly A. Driscoll.

emotion and interpretation. This step asks you (and this chapter will teach you) to identify and isolate your situational interpretations so that they can be more closely examined in subsequent steps of SA.

WHAT HAPPENS AT STEP 2?

Step 2 is very important, because you will not only learn how to identify your interpretations in a variety of situations but you also will begin to appreciate how these interpretations affect your interpersonal relationships and the outcomes of specific situations. Eventually, with practice using SA, identifying your interpretations during situations will become automatic. Your goal during Step 2 is to learn to construct relevant and accurate interpretations that can be examined during the remediation phase of SA (which is explained further in chapter 6).

At this point, you may be wondering what exactly is meant by an *interpretation.* Imagine that you have been passed over for a promotion at work or that you had yet another yelling match with your teenage daughter. Undoubtedly, you would have many thoughts and feelings during and after either of these frustrating situations. The *thoughts* you have *during the situation* are your interpretations. Interpretations are the thoughts we have about others and ourselves; they are the meaning that we attribute to such things as what people say to us, how people act toward us, and why certain things happen to us.

Interpretations can be specific or general, positive or negative. Many people have the tendency to make very general interpretations that are negative in nature. An example of a *general* negative interpretation is "My boss hates me"—a thought that could occur after an e-mail exchange in which you disagree with him or her about an aspect of a collaborative project. In contrast, an example of a *specific* negative interpretation is "My mother thinks that I am irresponsible when paying my bills" because you told her that you were late in paying last month's mortgage. It is important to stress that interpretations do not always have to be negative, and during the remediation of Step 2 (described in chapter 6) you will learn how to change your interpretations so that they are helpful to you. An example of a specific positive interpretation is "I had an enjoyable lunch with my brother this afternoon because we laughed the entire time."

WHY FOCUS ON STEP 2?

Learning to identify your interpretations of any given situation is a skill that has therapeutic benefits even independent of the other steps of SA. This is the only step that focuses explicitly on your thought processes—your personal "read" of a situation. This is not something most of us are accustomed to thinking about in any sort of systematic way. In fact, in many situations we encounter—particularly situations in which we are angry or otherwise extremely emotional—we may even feel as if we simply react automatically, without thinking at all. You may be able to think of examples of this experience from your own life. Somebody makes a comment to you, and you instantly become angry and snap back at him or her. Somebody gives you a certain look, and you are suddenly upset and tearful. Under such circumstances, our emotional and behavioral responses can appear to be instantaneous and reflexive; in fact, you may have felt at times that things would go better for you if you could only *think before acting*. Step 2 of SA emphasizes that you *are* thinking, in every situation, whether you realize it or not. It is your read of a situation—the meaning you assign to it—that leads you to become angry, tearful, excited, and so forth. Our emotions and our actions do not arise out of nowhere; they follow directly from the interpretations we make. We interpret a comment as insulting or intended to provoke, so we become angry and yell. We interpret a look as rejecting or hateful, so we become upset and cry. The examples are innumerable. The key point is that although it is true that our interpretations of a situation can happen so quickly as to barely be noticeable, they nonetheless have a tremendous influence on our behavior and, ultimately, on the outcomes of important situations in our lives. As such, there is great benefit in learning to identify your interpretations of important or stressful situations and to notice over time the patterns that may be leading to undesirable outcomes.

In this respect, the value of Step 2 is that it forces you to take a step back from the situation at hand and to notice what special sort of spin you were putting on that situation in your mind. Whereas the aim of Step 1 was to consider how a fly on the wall would have seen the situation, Step 2 moves the emphasis inside your head and asks you to answer the question "How did *you* read what was happening?" The goal at this point is not to question or evaluate the quality or appropriateness of your interpretations (that will come later) but rather simply to identify them—to recognize the way the situation looked through your eyes and to realize that this view is subjective and dependent on the particular interpretations that you made. It is important to realize that this process can be very tricky and can require lots of practice to master. Although the process of SA does not view your interpretations as being unconscious, repressed, or otherwise inaccessible to you, it is still the case that many of us are not used to paying attention to and noticing our own thoughts and "reads" of situations, particularly when they come to us at lightning-quick speed. We may recognize that we have a tendency to get angry or frustrated or discouraged quickly, but we may not be aware of the interpretations we are making that produce those emotions in us. One of the great benefits of SA is that it will teach you to attend to and keep track of the interpretations that you make—first in situations that have already occurred, and later in situations as they are unfolding. Even aside from the role this skill plays in the remainder of the SA steps, there is inherent benefit to be gained from this skill on its own. After practicing Step 2, you will become much more attuned to your own personal thought processes, and you will learn to recognize the patterns that characterize your way of viewing the world and the situations that arise in your day-to-day life.

However, although there are great benefits to be derived from mastering Step 2 on its own, there are far greater gains to be made from placing this step in the context of the rest of the SA process. As described earlier, it is in large part your interpretations that guide toward their ultimate outcomes the situations in which you find yourself. In the remaining steps of SA, you will be asked to specify your behaviors within the chosen situation, the outcome you desired for the situation (desired outcome [DO]), and the actual outcome (AO) of the situation. Each of these elements, as you will see, is largely determined by the interpretations you make at Step 2. Consider the example of a situation in which you lash out in anger in response to a comment made by someone else. It has already been stated that this emotional reaction and the resulting angry behavior (e.g., yelling, slamming doors, and even physical aggression) are the by-products of your interpretation of the situation, but how exactly does that work?

The key point to be learned in Step 2 is that any situation may be interpreted in a variety of ways. These different interpretations, in turn, are likely to produce vastly different behavioral reactions and, therefore, they contribute to vastly different situational outcomes. An illustrative example may help to clarify this point. Imagine that you are standing in line waiting to purchase lunch at a fast food restaurant, when you suddenly feel yourself bumped—hard—from behind. You ignore it at first, but then it happens again! How would you react? Many people, when presented with this situation, would indicate that at this point they might be getting frustrated, even angry. But let's add another detail: Imagine now that you turn around to see what is happening, and you discover a confused elderly person is standing behind you. Now how would you react? Most people, given this added detail, would indicate that they would no longer be angry—but why? The difference lies in the different interpretations of the situation. The way the situation was first presented, the anger or frustration many people would report feeling arises out of an interpretation that the shoving was intentional, or at the very least inconsiderate and careless. Believing that you had been deliberately pushed would likely lead you to feel angry and to react accordingly. However, if you were given some new information (e.g., the person who bumped into you was elderly and disoriented), that would likely result in your having a different interpretation of the same situation—namely, that your being pushed was an accident. This alternative interpretation would be far less likely to produce an angry reaction, although the precipitating events of the situation are the same in each case.

By learning to recognize your interpretations (and, with time and practice, the *patterns* in your interpretations), you will eventually understand where many of your more stressful situations may begin to go awry. By learning to step back and recognize that, first, you have a unique perspective on the events in your life and, second, that there could be other equally plausible perspectives on the exact same events, you will develop an awareness of your own thoughts that is absolutely central to effecting any sort of change through SA. The entire SA method rests on the underlying principle that we have control over the outcomes of meaningful situations in our lives and that we exert that control by tailoring our own thoughts and behaviors toward our preferred goals. However, before you can challenge, alter, or optimize your interpretations of a situation—and thus point yourself toward more helpful behaviors and better outcomes—you must be able to recognize and identify the interpretations that you make naturally. You will find that the effort put into Step 2 pays off in the end, in that you will hone your ability to notice the interpretations you make and to see the ways in which they contribute to your behaviors. At a later step, you will learn to analyze these interpretations in light of their contributions toward or away from your DOs, but at this juncture merely becoming skilled at identifying your interpretations constitutes a huge step toward improving both your own self-awareness and the outcome of multiple situations in your life.

ANDY AND BETH'S SITUATION

Let's consider the example of Andy's situation in which his fiancée, Beth, takes off for a Friday night out with friends without seeming to care that Andy is sitting home, alone, watching TV. You'll recall Andy's (revised and final) description of the situation from Chapter 2: "Beth told me that she was going to a club with her friends to dance and drink. She did not invite me to join them, but suggested that I hook up with some of my friends for a 'boys' night out.' I told her to have a good time." To complete Step 2 of SA using this situation, Andy must generate a short list of interpretations (3–4) he had during this situation. At first, Andy struggled to come up with this list—he tended to make feeling statements such as "I was really angry" or "My feelings were hurt." Although these are likely accurate statements about how Andy felt (and maybe still feels), they are not really interpretations that Andy had during the situation. Using a mental prompt of "What did it mean to me when Beth went out without me, seemingly unconcerned with my plans?" Andy was able to produce a list of his thoughts or interpretations that he had during the situation. The following is a list of Andy's interpretations:

1. Beth should have known that I would want her to invite me along.
2. I'm not going to tell her that I'm upset, because she will just get angry.
3. She'd rather hang out with her friends than me, like she doesn't even like me anymore.
4. She doesn't even care that I spent the whole night by myself—again.

The first three interpretations are ideal for use in SA because they are concise, they are thoughts rather than behaviors, they reflect Andy's thoughts rather than his emotions, they are directly tied to the situation, and they reflect what Andy thought while the situation was *in progress.* However, the fourth interpretation is one that Andy generated after the situation was over and is therefore not as useful. Keeping the interpretations limited to what you actually thought during the situation will enable you to determine how changing some of your thoughts while you were in the situation could have affected the overall outcome of the event for you. Therefore, Andy's revised list of interpretations would be the following:

1. Beth should have known that I would want her to invite me along.

2. I'm not going to tell her that I'm upset, because she will just get angry.
3. She'd rather hang out with her friends than me, like she doesn't even like me anymore.

COMMON STUMBLING BLOCKS

Although the process of identifying your interpretations during a given situation may seem simple enough, in fact, many people find it challenging. At first, you may find that you either have difficulty generating interpretations, or that you generate too many. If you are having difficulty generating interpretations, you can ask yourself a variety of questions to get yourself going in the right direction, including "At the time, when I was in the situation, it meant what to me?" You can also say to yourself, "When that happened, it meant ______ to me." For example, imagine that you are supposed to have dinner with a friend whom you have not seen in some time. As you are getting dressed, you realize that there is a message on your answering machine. Your friend has left a message canceling your dinner plans and stating briefly, "Something else has come up." You are disappointed because you were really looking forward to catching up with your friend; you are also hurt and decide to not call her back and instead spend the evening alone at home. You determine that this is a situation that you could plug into SA, but you experience difficulty generating interpretations. Therefore, to start the process, you might ask yourself, "When my friend canceled our dinner plans, it meant ______ to me." You could fill in the blank with, "She no longer wants to be my friend" or "She thinks I am dull and boring, and that is why she canceled our dinner plans." Asking yourself "What did this situation mean to me?" is just another way of asking, "What are my interpretations in this situation?", and this approach often facilitates the generation of interpretations.

Some people find that rather than struggling to come up with enough interpretations, they generate far too many interpretations. You may have this difficulty and feel that it is simply impossible to remember *all* the thoughts you had during a given situation. For example, consider the situation in which a mother is frustrated with her 8-year-old son's bad behavior in a restaurant while dining with her husband and some other friends. She may have many thoughts about the situation, including thoughts related to her ability to parent, her husband's willingness to help with parenting, her relationship with her husband, her son's irritating disposition, her own childhood, and even perhaps general thoughts about what makes a good parent. It clearly would be difficult for this woman to remember all of these thoughts. Fortunately, Step 2 does not require you to remember *all* your thoughts; rather, it asks you to choose the three or four that are most relevant. In fact, too many interpretations listed in SA can interfere with your ability to efficiently use this technique. If you find that you are generating too many interpretations during a specific situation, then simply limit yourself to three or four of your most powerful thoughts. A way to determine which thoughts are the most potent is to consider how you feel when you recall thinking a certain thought. If your emotions linked to a particular interpretation are especially strong, then that thought or interpretation is likely to be one that affects how you ultimately handled the situation, making it a viable option for consideration during your SA. Sometimes it can help to list as many interpretations as you can, rank them, and plug the top three or four into Step 2 of SA. With practice, you will eventually begin to notice patterns in your thinking, and the problematic interpretations that show up over and over in your SA will be the ones to concentrate on during this step.

Another obstacle that often interferes at this step is that people often state their feelings rather than interpretations. Although gauging how certain situations affect your emotions is important, this step asks you to focus on your *thoughts* rather than your *feelings* during the given situation. In fact, as previously mentioned, we believe that your *thoughts influence your emotions*, and therefore paying particular attention to the thoughts you automatically have during troubling situations will likely help you manage your emotions. Initially, it may be difficult to differentiate between your interpretations and your emotions. Many beginners in SA generate *emotion statements* rather than *interpretations*. Some examples of emotion statements are "It really made me angry when my boss expected me to work late again," "I just wanted to cry when she yelled at me," and "I was thrilled when he asked me out." Emotion statements are probably accurate reflections, and taking stock of how certain events make you feel is important, because feeling better is the essence of SA. However, this particular step asks you to focus on your thoughts, not on your emotions. Consider the example of a woman whose boss assumes for the fourth day in a row that she will stay after hours to work on a project. When asked to complete Step 2, she generates an emotion statement: "It really made me angry when my boss expected me to work late again." A revision of her emotion statement produces an *interpretation* of this same situation that is more useful in this step of SA, because it reflects what she thought during the situation: "My boss always takes advantage of me."

So far, we have given pointers that will help you as you complete Step 2 of SA. To clarify these and help you put them to use, we have created a worksheet to guide you through Step 2 (see Fig. 3.1). You do not need to use this worksheet each time you complete a SA, however, you may find it helpful in the beginning.

OTHER EXAMPLES

The following three examples help to further illustrate completion of Step 2.

Example 1

Julie has a 14-year-old daughter, Katherine, who is becoming increasingly sullen, moody, and socially isolated. Julie is worried about her and is frustrated by the arguments they seem to constantly have regarding Katherine's moody behavior and disinterest in socializing with friends. Julie decides to give the SA method a shot.

Step 1, the description of the situation, is as follows:

> Katherine and I had another argument. She decided to stay home Friday night even though her friends were all going to a movie. I told her she should go, and she became angry, and before long we were yelling at each other. She spent all night in her room, and I spent the whole evening angry and worried.

In her first try at Step 2, generating interpretations of the situation, Julie listed the following:

1. Katherine and I had a fight.
2. I shouldn't have argued with her.
3. I was very angry at Katherine.

As you may have noticed, this list of interpretations is not really a list of interpretations at all; rather, it is a series of statements that do not meet the criteria for Step 2. The first, "Katherine and I had a fight," is simply a statement of what happened rather than an interpretation. The second, "I shouldn't have argued with her," is a thought that Julie had *after* the situation occurred rather than an interpretation *during* the event. And the last

Worksheet for Step 2: Identifying Your Interpretations

1. First, generally describe in the space below what you thought was going on in the situation. When describing the situation in Step 1 of SA, you were asked to describe it as though you were a fly on the wall. Here, you want to describe it *through your own eyes,* focusing on what *you* thought about what was happening in the situation.

____

____

____

____

____

2. Identify, from what you just wrote, three or four interpretations for use in your SA. You must choose statements that meet certain criteria. To do this, ask yourself the following questions about each statement that you think you might use in your SA:

   A) Does your statement reflect something you *THOUGHT* rather than something you *DID*?

   B) Is your statement something you thought *DURING* the situation rather than *AFTER* the situation was over?

   C) Is your statement an *INTERPRETATION* rather than an *EMOTION STATEMENT*?

   If you answered "YES" to each of these questions about your statement, it is appropriate for use in Step 2 of SA. If not, try again using another statement or modify your existing statement to meet the above criteria.

3. List in the lines below all of the statements from what you wrote at the top of the page that meet the above criteria for Step 2. Then place a ranking of importance to the left of each statement (1= most important).

Rank	Interpretation
_____	_______________________________________
_____	_______________________________________
_____	_______________________________________
_____	_______________________________________
_____	_______________________________________
_____	_______________________________________
_____	_______________________________________

4. The top three or four are the interpretations you should now plug in to Step 2 of SA.

FIG. 3.1. Worksheet for Step 2: Identifying your interpretations. SA = Situational Analysis. Figure created by Karla K. Repper, Andrea B. Burns, and Kimberly A. Driscoll.

statement, "I was very angry at Katherine," is an *emotion statement* rather than an *interpretation.*

However, after completing the "Identifying Your Interpretations" worksheet (Fig. 3.1), Julie decided to alter her list of interpretations to the following:

1. Katherine will lose all her friends if she doesn't start hanging out with them more.
2. Katherine is becoming more and more unpleasant to be around.
3. I'm Katherine's mother, and I know she would feel better if she just went to the movie with her friends.

Each of these interpretations represents a thought Julie had during the situation and is perfect for use in her SA about the argument she had with Katherine.

Example 2

Mark was assigned to work on a project with a coworker, Tim. This involved being at another office, away from their supervisor, and the project had a strict timeline for completion. As they started the project together, Tim began to show up late to work, miss deadlines they had set, and leave work early. Tim disclosed that he was having marital difficulties and did not offer to make up work he missed or to let their supervisor know about his situation. Mark became increasingly frustrated and felt like he was being taken advantage of by Tim.

Step 1, the description of the situation, is as follows:

> Once again, Tim showed up three hours late to work even though we were supposed to meet to summarize our progress on the project and create a timeline for completion to give our boss by the end of the day. By the time he showed up, I had already finished the summary and had begun to work on the next step. Tim said he was sorry for being late and told a story about an argument he had with his wife. He then got on the phone and talked to his brother about the argument while I continued working.

In his first try at Step 2, generating interpretations of the situation, Mark listed the following:

1. I should have told him how I felt.
2. I was so frustrated I could have screamed.

3. I almost called my boss right then, but I chickened out.

Let's review why these statements do not work well in Step 2. The first one is a statement that Mark thought after the situation was over, but this step requires only thoughts that occurred during the situation. The second statement is an emotion statement, but this step requires statements that tell what Mark thought rather than what he felt. The third statement indicates what Mark did, and this step requires what he thought in this step, not what he did.

With appropriate alterations based on the worksheet in Fig. 3.1, Mark's final list of interpretations was the following:

1. Tim is a slacker, and I'm tired of doing his work for him.
2. I can't say anything to him or to my boss because I'd be a jerk for giving him a hard time when he's having trouble at home.
3. I think maybe I'm being taken advantage of.

These three interpretations all meet the criteria for use in Step 2 of SA.

Example 3

Carol's mother-in-law, Sarah, moved in with her and her husband approximately three years ago. Since that time, Carol has assumed almost all of the responsibility for Sarah, whose physical condition prevents her from cleaning, cooking, and bathing. Carol also takes Sarah to her doctor's appointments and to get her hair styled. Carol's husband, Rob, primarily dispenses his mother's medication, which is a complicated regimen. Carol's participation in volunteer activities has ceased, and she engages in very few leisure activities. She could not recall the last time she read a book for pleasure, something she loved to do. Carol began to feel like a prisoner in her own home and was becoming increasingly hopeless and depressed. Carol was becoming resentful of Sarah, which she demonstrated by being quite impatient when they interacted.

Step 1, the description of the situation, is as follows:

> I suggested to Rob that it might be time to consider making arrangements for Sarah to move into an assisted-living facility for older people. I explained that I was completely overwhelmed by the primary care responsibilities. Rob was completely supportive of the idea and thought that socialization at an assisted-care facility would be good for Sarah as well. However, I am con-

sumed by guilt and regret that I made the suggestion even though I know that it is in everyone's best interest.

In her first try at Step 2, generating interpretations of the situation, Carol listed the following:

1. I feel very guilty.
2. I shouldn't have said anything about Sarah moving out.
3. Rob said having Sarah move into a home was fine with him, but I don't think he means it.

As we have seen in the previous two case examples, this initial list of interpretations is problematic, because it contains statements that do not follow the rules of Step 2. The first statement is an emotion statement rather than a thought, and the other two statements are interpretations, but they were made after the situation occurred, rather than during the situation.

With the help of the worksheet in Fig. 3.1, Carol modified her list of interpretations to the following:

1. I am a terrible daughter-in-law.
2. Rob is just pacifying me temporarily. In the end he won't agree.
3. I owe it to Sarah to take care of her in my home. After all, she took care of Rob for all of those years; now it's our turn to take care of her.

These are all interpretations that are appropriate for use in Step 2 (keep in mind that in a later phase, remediation, these thoughts will be improved so that they are more likely to lead to DOs).

Although these three examples all have an initial list and a final list of interpretations, it is not necessary to construct both as you complete a SA. The initial lists in these examples were provided to illustrate common mistakes people make when completing Step 2. With practice, you will need to construct only one list of interpretations during this step.

SUMMARY AND CONCLUSIONS

As you have learned in this chapter, the second step of SA—identifying the interpretations you had during a given troubling situation—is a simple, but not necessarily easy, step to complete. However, mastering this step is essential. Identifying the thoughts you have in specific situations, especially situations that are problematic for you, is key to changing how you feel and handle things in general. This step is not only important within the overall context of SA: It has benefits all on its own. As you continue to learn the steps of SA and begin to practice it using situations from your own life, occasionally review this chapter and the examples to be sure you are on target with generating interpretations that are going to get you the most benefit from this process. Be patient! Most people tend to stumble a bit on this step at first. However, with a few reviews of the pointers offered in this chapter and some practice, you should quickly master Step 2 of SA.

Chapter 4

Step 3: Behaviors During the Situation*

As seen throughout this workbook, Situational Analysis (SA) is a multi-step process. Step 3 of this process is designed to focus on your behaviors during a given situation. This chapter outlines the step itself and describes how this step can be useful for you. Step 3 of Andy and Beth's situation will be presented so that you can see how this step worked in their case. Obstacles to successfully completing Step 3 will also be addressed, and examples are given to illustrate these points. After completing this chapter, you should be comfortable working through Step 3 of SA.

WHAT HAPPENS AT STEP 3?

Step 3 of SA consists of describing your behaviors during a specific situation. This might sound easy, but it might not be as straightforward as it sounds. For example, many people think that *behaviors* are only things that you said or actions you took in a situation, such as yelling "I hate you!" at someone and getting up and walking away after an argument. However, it is important to remember that your behaviors include much more than your words and actions in a given situation. Behaviors also include *how* you said what you said and *how* you did what you did. For example, what was your facial expression when you said or did it—were you smiling or

*The primary authors contributing to this chapter were Annya Hernandez and Jessica S. Brown.

scowling? What was your nonverbal body language—were you lying down relaxing in a lounge chair, or were your fists balled and your face red? Examples of nonobvious behaviors that you want to take note of for Step 3 include eye contact, tone of voice, body posture, facial expression, and timing. These nonobvious behaviors also communicate messages to others—sometimes as much, or more, than our words and actions.

Let us look at some more examples of behaviors during a situation that might not be obvious to you at first. Take eye contact, for example. Eye contact is an important component of communication. Looking someone in the eye while speaking communicates a different message than when you make little or no eye contact at all. Direct eye contact can convey self-confidence, authority, and intelligence, whereas no eye contact can convey embarrassment, discomfort, or deceit. Consider also your tone of voice: Was it angry, sad, or enthusiastic? Often what you say is not as important as how you say it. For example, telling someone that you love him or her in an angry tone of voice may send a mixed message. Another thing to notice is your body posture in situations. Were you facing the person? Did you have your arms crossed? Were you hunched over? Facing away from the person with whom you are speaking can communicate disinterest. Having an intimate conversation with your arms crossed can indicate to the person that you are not being open and sincere. Standing hunched over instead of upright may suggest that you are not feeling very confident. Actions and gestures during a situation also are important parts of behavioral communication and should be noticed and recorded during Step 3. Did you bang your fist on a desk? Did you slam a door? Did you cry? Gestures made while you are speaking can either strengthen or weaken the message you are communicating to another person. Another part of nonobvious communication is facial expression. For instance, if you are trying to be stern with your child but are also smiling, he might not understand that he is being punished. Finally, timing is also an important behavioral communicator in a conversation. Did you say things at an appropriate time? Did you respond quickly or slowly? All of these different nonverbal behaviors can communicate a great deal to others regarding your attitude, mood, and feelings. For example, pausing for a few seconds before responding can indicate that you are unsure about your answer, whereas answering someone immediately can indicate certainty and conviction. On the other hand, responding quickly to a question can suggest that you did not think over your answer, whereas responding slowly may suggest that you needed time to think it over.

WHY FOCUS ON STEP 3?

The purpose of Step 3 is to document in a given situation all your behaviors, including the nonobvious ones just discussed. You might be wondering why it is important to note your behaviors during the situation you described in Step 1. It is important to pay attention to and note your behaviors in situations because evaluating your behaviors can be a helpful way to improve your communication skills. Once you begin to do this, you may find that, in some situations, you did not communicate what you intended to. For example, perhaps you did not communicate everything that you wanted, or perhaps you communicated more than you intended. All behaviors, verbal and nonverbal, obvious and nonobvious, are important to consider because of the message that they send.

Although verbal and nonverbal behaviors can be documented independently of one another, it is important that you recognize that verbal and nonverbal behaviors work *together* to send a message. However, it is easy to see how they may combine to form mixed messages. Imagine you are trying to negotiate with someone—your boss, your spouse, your child, or a friend. You may be saying exactly what you mean to say, expressing your point in a very clear and convincing manner. You may even be saying it with a firm, strong tone of voice. But if you look nervous, avoid eye contact, and hesitate, the person you are talking to may sense some weakness and not take you seriously. However, it is easy to imagine that if you look confident, look the person directly in the eye, and speak without hesitation, you will appear much more confident, and a situation may turn out much differently.

It is the effect on the final outcome that makes this step an important part of the SA. The goal of Step 3 is to determine what you can do to make it more likely that you get what you want in everyday situations. Looking at your behaviors in a situation can provide opportunities for change so that you will get what you want the next time a similar situation comes along. Rather than looking at your behaviors in isolation, it is important to see them in the context of the entire situation. This will help you understand how your behaviors affected the outcome (i.e., were they helpful or hurtful?) and, if they had a negative effect, to modify them so they will be more helpful to you in future interpersonal situations.

Remember that Step 2 of SA is to identify your interpretations during a situation. Both what you say and how you say it is influenced by your interpretation of a situation. When you use SA to record your thoughts and your behaviors, it is easier to see the interaction between the two. Furthermore, as you progress through this workbook, you will see that future steps ask you to identify how a situation turned out and how you would have liked for it to turn out. This process allows you to see how your behaviors during a situation contributed to the outcome that resulted. Recognizing how your behaviors influence the outcome of a situation is a key component to being able to bring about the outcomes that you want.

ANDY AND BETH'S SITUATION

As you will recall from previous chapters, Beth and Andy began having difficulties after they got engaged. Andy feels that he is an easy person to get along with and does not understand Beth's constant agitation with him. He also feels that she does not understand his feelings of rejection and loneliness. Focusing on Step 3 in Andy's SA might shed some light on the problem. On his SA worksheet, Andy described his behaviors as follows:

1. All I said was for her to have fun. I didn't ask her if I could come along.
2. My tone of voice was "defeated"—I didn't sound happy with her when she left.
3. I wouldn't look at her or smile—I just sort of ignored her and watched TV.
4. When she came home, I was very quiet and didn't really respond when she told me how much fun she had.

The first three behaviors generated by Andy are ideal for use in SA, because they are descriptions of both verbal ("All I said was for her to have fun") and nonverbal ("I wouldn't look at her or smile . . .") behaviors. Andy also included some nonobvious behaviors in his SA—his tone of voice, for example. In addition, the first three behaviors are ideal for SA because they are what occurred while the situation was *in progress*. The fourth behavior is one that Andy generated *after* the situation was over and is therefore not as useful in this SA. Keeping the behaviors limited to what you did or said during the situation will enable you to determine how changing some of your behaviors while you were in the situation could have affected the overall outcome of the event for you. Therefore, Andy's revised list of behaviors would be the following:

1. All I said was for her to have fun. I didn't ask her if I could come along.
2. My tone of voice was "defeated"—I didn't sound happy with her when she left.
3. I wouldn't look at her or smile—I just sort of ignored her and watched TV.

COMMON STUMBLING BLOCKS

People sometimes experience difficulty with Step 3 because they don't pay much attention to their behaviors. For example, you may not be used to thinking of your behaviors as comprising a number of discrete verbal and nonverbal elements. Instead, you may just see it all as being one big behavior. Step 3 requires you to break up your behavior into smaller parts to analyze whether these parts were helpful or hurtful to you in getting your desired outcome in later SA steps (this is explained further in subsequent chapters). Looking at past situations through SA can help you begin to get used to breaking apart your behavior in a situation to see all of its elements. Also, you can use Fig. 4.1 as a helpful worksheet for completing Step 3. This worksheet requires you to list out all verbal and nonverbal behaviors in a situation, so it can be particularly helpful when you are first learning how to complete Step 3, because it reminds you what to look for in your behaviors during a situation.

Another common stumbling block is making sure the behaviors you list in Step 3 are tied to the situation described in Step 1. You saw how Andy had a problem with this in his initial list of behaviors in Step 3. It is important for the behaviors listed to reflect the discrete slice of time described in Step 1 (see chapter 2).

A final stumbling block is that people sometimes believe that they have to list only their negative behaviors in a situation. This is incorrect: The important part of Step 3 is that you list a few of the most important behaviors, whether they seem positive or negative to you. Just list what your behaviors were in the given situation. Analyzing their helpfulness comes later. It is as important to consider positive behaviors as it is negative behaviors, because that will help you decide later what works for you and what does not work for you (this same point applies to Step 2, on interpretations).

Worksheet for Step 3: Behaviors During the Situation

Think of a situation you have been working on. Now think of your behavior in that situation. Note the following:

What you said: ____

____

____

What you did: ____

____

____

Tone of voice: ____

____

____

Timing: ____

____

____

Body Posture: ____

____

____

Facial Expression: ____

____

____

Eye Contact: ____

____

____

FIG. 4.1. Worksheet for Step 3: Behaviors During the Situation. Figure created by Annya Hernandez and Jessica S. Brown.

OTHER EXAMPLES

The following examples might help to further illustrate completion of Step 3.

Example 1

Susan had dozens of regular customers who always returned to the restaurant for her prompt service and warm disposition. However, Susan never seemed to get a raise from her boss. In fact, she even got fired. Susan did not understand the reasons for this and consulted her therapist about it. She told her therapist about the situation: "The cash register was short. My boss asked me why this happened. I told him I didn't know, and he fired me." On her SA worksheet Susan described her behaviors as follows:

1. I told my boss that I did not know why the register was short.
2. I stayed quiet while he was questioning me.

Susan does a great job at generating her verbal behaviors during the situation. However, Susan's list does not include all the nonverbal behaviors she demonstrated during her interaction with her boss. Thus, Susan's revised list of behaviors would be the following:

1. I told my boss that I did not know why the register was short.
2. I stayed quiet while he was questioning me.
3. I got nervous and didn't answer immediately.
4. I looked at my feet instead of at my boss.

Example 2

Abigail felt her teacher did not give her the grade she deserved. Even though, much like Susan, talking to her teachers made Abigail very nervous, she acted in a different way. Abigail worked very hard on her term paper and was very saddened when her teacher gave her a C. Her teacher wrote that the report seemed incomplete and that she expected more participation from Abigail in class. Although Abigail wanted to run away and cry, she decided to stand up for herself and talk to her teacher. Later, she told her therapist what happened. "I got a bad grade on my paper. I met with my teacher about changing my grade. We talked and she said she would not change it. I stormed out of the classroom." On her SA worksheet Abigail described her behaviors as follows:

1. I stormed out of the classroom.
2. I didn't look the teacher in the eye.
3. My fists were balled up.

Abigail paid a great deal of attention to her nonverbal behaviors; however, she forgot to list her verbal behaviors. Her list should include both, because it is equally important to be aware of what you say and how you say it. So, a more complete list, including her verbal and nonverbal behaviors, would be:

1. I stormed out of the classroom.
2. I didn't look the teacher in the eye.
3. My fists were balled up.
4. I told her this was unfair in an angry tone of voice.

Example 3

Another common problem people run into with Step 3 is making sure their behaviors are tied to the discrete slice of time described in Step 1. For example, Danny has a son who tries to be helpful but who often gets into trouble. One day, the son came home from school and decided he wanted to surprise his parents by cleaning up the office. He took all of the messy groups of papers in the office and put them into one neat pile on the desk. Delighted with his tidy assistance, Danny's son was very confused and surprised when his parents yelled loudly at him when they got home. Apparently, they had spent the whole weekend separating all the documents they needed to complete their taxes the following day. Danny later told his therapist about the situation: "I got home after a long day and found our tax documents all in one pile. I yelled at my son and told him to go to his room." On his SA worksheet, Danny described his behaviors as follows:

1. I yelled at my son loudly and told him to go to his room.
2. My cheeks were red, and I felt hot.
3. I looked straight into his eyes.
4. I always tell him not to touch our things.

Danny's list is ideal for SA, because it included both his verbal and nonverbal behaviors that occurred during the specific slice of time described in Step 1. However, his fourth behavior is one that, although he may do often, he did not do in this situation. Thus, it was not helpful to include the fourth one in his list. A more appropriate list, including behaviors that occurred only in that situation would be:

1. I yelled at my son loudly and told him to go to his room.
2. My cheeks were red, and I felt hot.
3. I looked straight into his eyes.

Keep in mind, of course, that these behaviors will be evaluated as to whether they were helpful or not in attaining desired outcomes (DOs)—but we haven't gotten to that step yet.

Example 4

Focusing only on one type of behavior, good or bad, is another stumbling block of Step 3. Take Harry, for example. He was a hard-working security guard who loved his wife very much. However, their arguments seemed to be increasing since he had changed to the morning shift. Every morning, he woke up and made a list of things he wanted to talk to his wife about before he left for work. His wife, Brenda, was a nurse who worked the night shift. So, every morning when Brenda arrived from work, Harry was waiting with his list of things to talk about. Even though she loved Harry very much, Brenda felt like he was bombarding her with issues when she was tired. All she wanted to do was give him a kiss goodbye and crawl into bed. Harry told his therapist about the latest argument with Brenda. "When she came home, I told Brenda that I wanted to talk about what needed to be done around the house. She said we'd talk later. I said that we never talk when I want to, and I left for work." On his SA worksheet Harry described his behaviors as follows:

1. I told Brenda that we never talk when I want to.
2. My tone was angry.

Harry focused only on his negative behaviors, the ones he was not proud of. To have a more complete list of behaviors, Harry needed to include both the negative and the positive things he did and said in the situation. Thus, his revised list would be:

1. I told Brenda that we never talk when I want to.
2. My tone was angry.
3. I looked straight into her eyes.
4. I faced Brenda when I was talking to her.

Example 5

Brenda had the same problem that Harry did. She focused on only one type of behavior while she made her list for Step 3. She told her therapist about the same situation. "I got home from work, and Harry wanted to talk about what needed to be done around the house. I said we'd talk later. He then said that we never talked when he wanted to and left for work." On her SA worksheet Brenda described her behaviors as follows:

1. I told Harry that we'd talk later.
2. My tone was neutral.

Unlike Harry, but equally problematic, Brenda focused only on her positive behaviors. She did not report any negative behaviors that she engaged in during the situation. To have a more complete list of behaviors, Brenda (just like Harry) needed to include both the negative and the positive things she did and said in the situation. Thus, her revised list would be:

1. I told Harry that we'd talk later.
2. My tone was neutral.
3. I rolled my eyes when Harry was speaking to me.
4. I plopped on the couch, under a blanket, when I was talking to Harry.

SUMMARY AND CONCLUSIONS

Although Step 3 can be a little tricky to master, once you have done so it is very helpful in getting what you want in a situation. When your behaviors match what you are feeling and thinking, things go better. Remember, Step 3 focuses on the behaviors engaged in during a given situation. When your eye contact, posture, tone of voice, timing, words, and actions are all in sync with what you want, you are more likely to obtain your DO. Remember to use the worksheet for Step 3 in Fig. 4.1.

Chapter 5

Steps 4 and 5: Desired and Actual Outcomes*

In general, the purpose of Situational Analysis (SA) is to help you get what you want. This chapter breaks down this process into two steps: (a) the desired outcome (DO) and (b) the actual outcome (AO). It can be frustrating, and sometimes downright depressing, when we never get what we want out of life (i.e., the DO), so our purpose here is to get systematic about closing the gap between the AO and DO so that eventually you can get *what you want* out of most situations.

STEP 4: THE DESIRED OUTCOME

We refer to Step 4 of SA as the "magic wand" step, because you are going to ask yourself the following question: "If I had a magic wand that I could wave and have the situation turn out any way that I wanted, *this* is what I would have happen." Sounds pretty nice, doesn't it? But there are a few catches. This magic wand cannot change the behavior of other people, and it cannot break the laws of physics or nature. We discuss this further later in the chapter.

Before describing the DO in greater detail, however, let's establish why this step is so important. Oftentimes, the notion that you can truly get what *you* want (as opposed to getting what other people give you) is an

*The primary authors contributing to this chapter were J. Anthony Richey, Sheila L. Stanley, and Lindsey Kirsch.

empowering idea. It makes good sense, too, that the more you get what you want out of life, the better you will feel. Consider, for instance, the issues that are troubling you now. Whatever they might be, chances are that some, if not all, problems stem from a discrepancy between what you want and what you have, which causes distress and frustration. Generally speaking, it is hard to get what you want if you aren't clear about what it is that you want. Once you figure out what you would like, you can determine how to think and act to get it. Therefore, the DO is the keystone of SA, because you will work toward making the DO a reality.

What Happens at Step 4?

What is a DO, and how do you generate it? Our purpose here is to guide you through the process of generating a *realistic* and *attainable* DO. The first thing to do is ask the "magic wand" question: "If I could wave a magic wand and have the situation turn out any way I wanted, I would have wanted ______." The answer to this question is your DO. Remember, though, that this magic wand is not all-powerful. There are a few restrictions to what it can do. First, it can't change the behavior of others. The DO should *not* sound something like this: "I would have really wanted my boss to just go and fire my annoying coworker." Second, this wand cannot change the laws of nature or physics. For example: "I would have wanted to go back in time and not pick up the phone when my mother called." A DO like this won't help you, so don't bother. Apart from these two rules, the rest is pretty much up to you. Be warned, however: Some DOs are better than others. The following acronym (SUPERB) will help you remember six simple rules for generating a usable DO.

A good DO will be:

1. Short
   a. If your DO is more than one sentence, it is too long.
   b. No cheating with run-on sentences, either (and then I want this, then that, then this . . . etc.)!
   c. An example of a good, one-sentence DO is something like this: "I wanted to resist eating that dessert that I really didn't need."
2. Unchanging
   a. Once you decide on a good DO, don't change it.
   b. It is not a good idea to go back and revise your goals. Pick what you want and stick with it. In the later steps of SA, especially the remediation phase, this becomes important.

3. Precise
   a. Be as specific as you possibly can.
   b. A DO that is too broad (e.g., "I just want to feel better") is not as good as one that is anchored to your slice of time and extremely specific (e.g., "I wanted to express my anger toward my husband yesterday when he screamed at me").
4. Elementary
   a. Oftentimes, people come up with DOs that are way too complicated. You want a DO that is simple.
   b. You are only trying to come up with a short-term goal, so your DO should not stretch out over time (i.e., it should not exceed the time boundaries of your slice of time), and it should not require so many steps that no human being would be able to complete them all (e.g., "I wanted to be smarter, so that I can get my work done faster, so I can have more time to spend with my wife and she doesn't nag on me that I am not spending enough time with her and that I am a workaholic").
   c. Therefore, have only one or at the most two steps in your DO (e.g., "I wanted to tell her I love her, and that I will leave an hour early Friday to spend time with her").
5. Ranked
   a. This rule is important only if you have more than one DO.
   b. Remember, in SA you should have one and only one DO.
   c. If you really do have more than one, and you just can't decide which to use, *rank them* in order of importance.
   d. The DO that is most important is the one that you would most like to see happen. Pick that one and only that one.
6. Behavioral
   a. The best DOs are the ones that are constructed in *behavioral* terms.
   b. This is one of the most important and sometimes the most difficult aspect of generating a DO.
   c. It is definitely okay to have a "thought" component to your DO (e.g., "I wanted to believe I was competent and hard working"). However, people sometimes want to construct a DO in only emotional terms (e.g., "My goal is to become less upset by my laziness"). Try to find the actual behavior or thought that accompa-

nies the emotion; thus, the previous example might become: "My goal is to get out of bed on time tomorrow morning."

d. The reason for this is discussed in detail later, but for now just remember that your emotions will follow your behavior.

So, we have two sets of guidelines: (a) the unbreakable rules of the magic wand and (b) the SUPERB principles. The former are non-negotiable, but the SUPERB principles are a little more flexible. Follow these principles closely, and you will likely come up with a DO that is both realistic and within reach. If, however, you are finding that the DO that you generate is just not working, follow these simple rules for revision.

Revision Rules

If the environment cannot deliver your DO, and/or you do not have the ability to produce your DO, it must be revised. This typically happens when one or more of the preceding rules are violated, so get in the habit of going through the SUPERB principles. A worksheet is presented in this chapter (Fig. 5.1) to help you determine whether you have a usable DO or if you need to go back and revise before moving on to the next step of SA. Keep revising until your DO fits within the constraints of the rules outlined earlier.

Why Focus on Desired Outcomes?

One of the interesting things about SA is that each step by itself has the power to help you feel more positive and in control. If you were to focus on the DO and the DO alone, you would begin to experience relief. This is because goal-oriented thinking is a powerful tool in feeling more positive. The fact of the matter is, though, that most people do not think in terms of their own goals. You can probably imagine challenging situations you have walked into, say at work or school, where you "went through the motions" and came out on the other side of the situation feeling frustrated, anxious, or even depressed. What if you had had a clear goal in mind when you went into that situation? Would that have given you a new perspective and a clearer sense of how to act?

If you believe the answer is "yes," then you have a pretty good sense of why this kind of thinking is so helpful. The feeling that you are floating around with no clear sense of direction can be an upsetting one. This feel-

Elicitation Phase of Step 4

STEP 4: The Desired Outcome (DO)

1) Complete this sentence: "If I could wave a magic wand in my situation, I would have wanted . . . ____
____
____."

2) Check your DO

Does it attempt to directly control the behavior of others? Yes____ No____

Does it violate the laws of physics or nature? Yes____ No____

If both answers are no, continue.

The SUPERB principles

Is your DO . . .

SHORT	____	**Yes, I have only one sentence.**
	____	No, there is more than one sentence.
UNCHANGING	____	**Yes, after any revisions I will stick with this DO.**
	____	No, I might have to change it in later steps of SA.
PRECISE	____	**Yes, it's very specific and anchored to my slice of time.**
	____	No, my DO is phrased in broad terms.
ELEMENTARY	____	**Yes, it has only one or two steps.**
	____	No, there are more than two steps.
RANKED	____	Not necessary. I had only one DO.
	____	**Yes, I had multiple DOs and chose the one I would most like to see happen.**
BEHAVIORAL	____	**Yes, my DO is framed in terms of behaviors.**
	____	No, my DO is more emotion based.

If you marked the boldface answers, you have a usable DO and you should continue to the next step in SA. Be sure to also consider:

1) Does my DO occur strictly within my slice of time?
2) Is my DO clearly helpful to me?

FIG. 5.1. Elicitation phase of Step 4. Figure created by J. Anthony Richey, Sheila L. Stanley, and Lindsey Kirsch.

ing is what the DO is usually able to defeat on its own. Chances are, if you used only this step, you would figure out on your own how to achieve your DO. However, if you are like most people, you don't have time to wait around. You want to feel better *now.*

This is why you should embed your goal in a system like SA, which teaches you how to systematically evaluate how your behavior adds or subtracts to hitting that bull's-eye of your DO. Eventually, you will be an expert at modifying your own behavior so that you can accomplish your goals every time. If you do this, your recovery will be much faster and last longer than if you did this step alone.

Andy and Beth's Situation

Let's take a look at the case of Andy and Beth as an example. On the basis of what you have learned so far, see if you can pinpoint what Andy does wrong.

Andy's DO

> I wanted her [Beth] to want me to come along. I wanted her to realize that she's being rude by leaving me out and making me feel rejected.

Problems With Andy's DO

1. It breaks one of the magic wand rules. The magic wand cannot change the behavior of other people. When Andy says what he wanted Beth to do, he is creating a DO based on altering others. We cannot count on changing others, but we can count on changing our own actions. Remember to create a DO that focuses on *you.*
2. It is too long. One sentence would be ideal.

To see how Andy's DO could be better, stop for a second and think about the SUPERB principles. The DO should be anchored to the situation, should obey the magic wand rules, and should be stated in one sentence.

Andy's Revised DO

"I wanted to stand up for myself by telling her I felt rejected and lonely when she left me out of her plans tonight."

Common Stumbling Blocks and Other Examples

As you go through the process of generating a DO, there are a few common hurdles that you might come up against. This section will help you by dividing them up into frequently asked questions (FAQs) that you might have and common problems in coming up with a usable DO.

- FAQ #1: *My problem feels like it's more emotional than anything else. How will creating a goal work to change my emotions?*

This is one of the most common questions asked regarding Step 4 and sometimes of SA in general. The idea is this: When you have a goal, you have a clear end point for your behavior. Think of it as being like a roadmap, with the DO as your destination. If you have no destination in mind when you leave your house in the morning, driving around all day not sure where you are going (and not sure if you even get there) sounds like a frustrating and distressing experience that could go on for weeks, months, or even years. This distress often transforms into an array of general negative emotions. So, it's pretty logical that you can avoid this emotional distress by not only setting a goal, but also setting a *desirable* goal.

- FAQ #2: *What's the point of coming up with a DO for an event that already happened? It's not like I can actually go back and change how that situation came out.*

You're right—you can't go back in time and change things, but this is not what SA is asking you to do. We want you to think this way about *past* situations, so that when another one comes up, you will be able to use SA to navigate it as the situation unfolds.

- FAQ #3: *Well, if I want to hit my DO right on the bull's-eye every time, I should be constructing pretty easy goals, right?*

Actually, easy DOs are not always helpful. Your DO should be a bit challenging for you. If you consistently challenge yourself by constructing goals that are just slightly outside of your comfort zone, then your recovery will be greatly accelerated. If, on the other hand, you select goals that are safe, and not challenging, your progress may be slowed.

- Common Problem #1: Nonbehavioral DOs

This is perhaps the most common problem in Step 4. Because the source of your particular problem might have an emotional component (i.e., anger, embarrassment, nervousness, etc.), it is sometimes tempting to target this first, because it is the most distressing. It is okay to have an emotional component to your DO (e.g., "I wanted to assert myself *and not feel ashamed*"), but it is absolutely essential that you have a behavioral component as well. In the previous example, the words in italic type represent the emotional component of this imaginary DO, but note how there is a behavioral aspect to the DO as well. A good way to combat this common hurdle is to think about your magic wand giving you the power to *behave* in a certain way.

• Common Problem #2: Unhelpful DOs

We've been discussing getting what you want. What if you do get what you want every time, but you still feel distressed? Your DO might be unhelpful. Consider this example:

Client (C): My DO was to stay in bed all day.

Therapist (T): And you got what you wanted?

C: Right.

T: That's interesting . . . you got your DO, but you still feel upset. What do you make of that?

C: Sounds like I need a better DO.

T: I agree. That one didn't sound particularly helpful. Can you revise it?

C: Well, in a perfect world, I wouldn't have wanted to stay in bed all day, and then I would have been motivated to get up.

T: Great. It sounds like that is more helpful, and there is a clear "thought" component to your DO that we can work with, too.

In this example, the client met all the principles we suggested, and got what he wanted. However, the DO simply did not help him in his recovery, so he had to revise it. If you suspect your DO is not helpful, ask yourself "Does this DO get me closer to my recovery, or is it just the status quo?" This might take a little practice, but start to think about goals that would *really* give you some relief. The following are more examples of individuals using SA and learning to formulate DOs using the steps we've described here:

Matthew's situation: Well, I was shuffling through some papers on my desk Thursday night after work. I can't remember what I was looking for, but I'll tell you what I found. I found a letter, addressed to one of Sara's ex-boyfriends! I couldn't believe it! I held onto the letter, and wanted to open it, but didn't. I decided to confront Sara about it first. But, when Sara came home I didn't really speak to her. She asked me to eat dinner with her. I told her I already ate, and I was very busy. I sat at the desk by myself.

Matthew's DO: Well, if I had a magic wand I would have waved it over that letter, and poof, it would be gone! And so would my bad feelings.

Therapist: I understand you wanting that to happen. That would be nice. Then the situation would not have arisen at all. But remember what we talked about last time? There are certain things the wand can't do. It can't change other people's behavior, and it can't alter the laws of physics. So, you can't just make things disappear. So, revise your DO and try to think about the SUPERB principles as you do it.

Matthew's revised DO: I don't see what the good is of a magic wand, if it can't poof things away. . . . But, I guess I see what you are getting at. When things do happen, I need to know—realistically—what I want. OK, so what I wanted was to be happy and secure in my relationship with Sara. I love her. I don't want to feel jealous anymore about anything. I just want to feel confident that she loves me too.

Let's stop here for a second. There is still something wrong with Matthew's revised DO. Can you pinpoint what it is? First of all, the DO needs to be *short.* Second, this DO is not *precise.* It is very broad and not specific to the situation. If you get stuck here, try to think of something that can be accomplished right then and there. Also, it is very important to include *behavioral* terms in your DO. This way, the targets are things you can do to change the situation the way you want. If you find this an obstacle, and can think only of changing your emotions, remember to try thinking of the behavior that accompanies the emotion. After the therapist talked these things over with Matthew, he came up with a new DO.

Matthew's final DO: I wanted to be assertive with Sara and discuss the fact that writing to her ex made me upset and jealous.

Therapist: Excellent DO. Do you see how this gives you an attainable goal that is much better than the broad statement you came up with before? In a single situation like this one, it would be difficult to solve all of the relationship problems, and feel completely happy and secure. Instead, we take it step by step—one situation at a time.

Anna's situation: I was in my car yesterday and this woman cut me off on the highway. I guess I shouldn't have let it bother me, but I just got so mad. I couldn't stop thinking about it, even after I got to work. I kept playing it over and over in my head and what I should have done. It would have felt so good to lay on that horn, nice and loud, or flip her off while I sped past her. It was a few hours later before I could really let it go. I felt like such a wimp.

Anna's DO: Well, I guess I would have wanted to show her how mad I was.

Therapist (T): So your DO was to show your anger somehow?

Anna (A): Right.

T: That's interesting, because even beyond being simply angry, you said that you felt frustrated and like a wimp.

A: Exactly! It's just another example of how I can never stand up for myself, and when I get like that, I just can't let it go. I can't stop thinking about how weak I am.

T: So let's be critical here. Was your DO really to honk your horn, or was it to feel less frustrated and not ruminate for hours?

A: Maybe. Honking the horn would have gotten some aggression out, that's for sure.

T: So, you would have released some aggression. If that had been the case, would you have ruminated about the incident for the next few hours?

A: Hmm—now that I'm not sure of. I guess I might have played it over in my mind whether I honked or not. I can see myself worrying about it no matter what I did. I really just wanted to forget about it and go about my business, more than anything else.

T: So how can you revise your DO to reflect the desire to "let it go" and continue with your day?

A: I would have wanted to see the other driver for what they were, which was an inconsiderate fool, instead of blaming myself for being victimized, when the situation wasn't even my fault.

T: Good. We can work with that.

Step 4 Conclusion

To wrap up our discussion of Step 4, the two general principles (the magic wand laws and the SUPERB guidelines) will guide you through the process of generating a workable DO. If it seems complicated right now, don't worry. With a little practice this will become second nature to you.

STEP 5: ACTUAL OUTCOME

In working through SA, you have performed several steps thus far, including selecting a discrete slice of time (Step 1), describing what the situation meant to you (Step 2), describing how you behaved in the situation (Step 3), and describing how you wanted the situation to turn out (Step 4). The next step of SA offers a glimpse of how it all fits together. We refer to this step as the AO. This step is simply a concrete description of what *actually* happened. In other words, the AO ends the time sequence that you initiated in Step 1. The goal of this step is to generate a descriptive statement that accurately reflects the end of the time sequence in the described situation. Generating a statement about how an event turned out seems to be a simple, straightforward task; however, in practice this is not always the case. In any given situation involving interpersonal interactions, it is possible to select from among several stopping points, such that the selection of any one may seem arbitrary. However, it rarely is arbitrary, and to gain the most benefit from this exercise, you will want to carefully consider which stopping point you select.

What Happens at Step 5?

A good AO statement contains three essential components:

1. It represents the end of the time line in the described situation.
2. It is clear and accurately reflects what actually took place in the situation.
3. Like the DO, the AO should be expressed in behavioral, not emotional terms.

When the AO contains all three of these components, you have been successful in objectifying a situation. It is important to note that an objective assessment does not mean the absence of an emotional response; however, because emotional responses are often the result of how successful or unsuccessful we are in any situation, they are considered only in conjunction with behavioral outcomes and never in isolation.

Developing an accurate AO places you in a better position to see how what you think and how you behave in any given situation largely influence the way the situation turns out for you. Objective assessment is a learned skill, and it improves with practice. Initially, you may find it difficult to use this skill while in a live situation, but don't worry—with a little practice, this process will become automatic.

Why Focus on Actual Outcomes?

One interesting aspect of thinking about AOs is that it gives you a tool to clearly and accurately assess what is occurring in a systematic and objective way, and this can be therapeutic on its own. Consider, for example, socially phobic individuals, who often fear negative evaluation by others. This feared situation often does not exist in reality, but the socially phobic individual can't see that, because he or she doesn't have the skill to step back from the situation and see it for what it is. This skill is an explicit component of the AO, which requires you to make an objective and accurate assessment of a situation based on the observable facts. The AO clearly will benefit socially anxious people whose negative emotions often impede objectivity, but it will also benefit anyone who finds it difficult to step back and see what is really going on in a given situation.

The following excerpt is an exchange with a client who was diagnosed with social phobia and clearly illustrates this point. In this situation, the client had gone to the movies on a Friday evening and had been concerned that everyone would notice that he was alone and conclude that he was a "loser." Notice that the client provides both an emotional response as well as a behavioral outcome. Again, this is permissible, especially in this case, as it highlights the link between successful events and positive emotions.

> *Therapist:* So, what was the AO?
>
> *Client:* I got in my car and went to the movies. I tried to feel brave, and I ended up feeling pretty good, too, because I got out there and did something adventurous. I thought it would just be like a real hurricane, you know? I wondered if people would look at me, but I noticed that they didn't. They were pretty much involved in their own stuff.

In this example, the idea of going to the movies was a frightening prospect for this client, because it was clearly overwhelming. When broken down into its component parts (getting in the car, driving to the movies, watching the film, etc.), however, the AO of going to the movies alone was not as overpowering an experience as he might have thought. So, in this capacity, Step 5 may also help individuals who have very chaotic lives. In fact, you might think of times when you have had difficulty delineating where one situation stops and another starts. The ability to step back from it all, even a little, may help you slow life down a bit and cut it into small snippets, thereby making life seem much more manageable.

Andy and Beth's Situation

Let's check back in with Andy. Andy's AO, taken from the running case presentation, has a couple of problems that the therapist might work through in the following manner:

Andy (A): We got into an argument when Beth came home. She told me I make her feel guilty by "pouting" and said that she just needed some space to be on her own. I just let it go and went to sleep on the couch, but I felt awful. She just seemed agitated with me.

Therapist (T): I am a bit confused on a couple of points. You say that you and Beth argued when she came home. I'm not sure whether that is the AO of the earlier situation, or if it is the beginning of a different situation. Also, it is important that you remember to keep the AO to one or two sentences at most and that you only talk about behaviors.

A: Well I'm not really sure that I can separate the two situations. On the one hand, I sat at home watching TV on a Friday night while she went out and had fun, but we did argue when she got home, which also made me feel bad.

T: I do see how this can be confusing, and both of these outcomes are important. Is either of these more reflective of your typical way of interacting with her?

A: Yeah, I think the first, because lately I spend a lot of time alone at home while she goes out.

T: So the AO in this situation is that you stayed at home alone on Friday night while your fiancée went out, and you felt miserable.

A: Yeah, I'd say that is accurate.

You will note that Andy's outcome initially contained several possible outcomes that spanned several hours. This is not ideal because it increases the possibility that more than one situation will present itself—which is what occurred in Andy's case. Remember that the AO will be at the end of a discrete slice of time. In addition, Andy included his evaluation of what his fiancée was feeling—"She was just agitated with me"—which violates the behavioral requirement of a good AO. The final AO clearly contains all three components of a good AO: (a) it demarcates a discrete slice of time, (b) it is clear and accurate, and (c) it is expressed in behavioral terms. Once the AO is developed, it is best not to change it in subsequent steps, so it is worth spending the time early on to develop a good one.

The AO is the step most likely to be overlooked, in part because it seems so superficially straightforward. McCullough (2000), however, described this as the pivotal step in recognizing consequences and identifying how our cognitions and behaviors affect these outcomes. Also, it is the event that specifies the end of our slice of time and, as such, is as important as the starting point in structuring how we think about situations.

Remember that your AO must represent the end point of your slice of time, it must reflect what actually happened (not your interpretation of what happened), and it must be behaviorally framed (see Fig. 5.2).

Elicitation Phase of Step 5

STEP 5: The Actual Outcome (AO)

Now that you have established what you would have *wanted* to happen, the next question is: What *actually* happened?

Write your AO in the space below.

____

____

____

____

____

____

IF . . .

1) The AO is *not* the same thing as the end point of your slice of time . . .
2) The AO is based on your interpretation of an event, rather than the actual event . . .
3) The AO is *not* framed in behavioral or cognitive terms . . .

. . . then you must revise. If necessary, write your revised AO in the space below.

____

____

____

____

____

____

FIG. 5.2. Elicitation phase of Step 5. Figure created by J. Anthony Richey, Sheila L. Stanley, and Lindsey Kirsch.

Common Stumbling Blocks and Other Examples

John's Original AO

After our argument, I stormed out the door and just kept driving around all night long. I returned home the next morning, and, of course, she was mad as hell and started in on me again.

There are several problems with this AO. First, it clearly does not meet the short slice of time criterion, as it encompasses a huge chunk of time beyond the end of the interaction (i.e., the argument). Remember that the AO must clearly demarcate the end of the situation, and in general the AO and the end of situation are one and the same. Second, because the AO does not clearly define the end point of the first situation, it allows one situation to merge right into another related, but separate, situation.

John's Revised AO

After our argument, I stormed out the door.

Gregory's Original AO

I made a complete fool of myself. I'm sure she thinks I'm a loser and will never take my phone calls again. Man, how embarrassing.

Gregory is engulfed in his emotional response to the situation, and he has not indicated any behavioral outcomes. Furthermore, it is an inaccurate assessment of what occurred in the situation. Negative emotions often cloud our ability to make clear objective observations, and so these two errors frequently co-occur. A good AO must be framed behaviorally, so although it is permissible for Gregory to add that he felt embarrassed because of a particular behavior, that feeling cannot stand on its own.

Gregory's Revised AO

She said that she had already made plans for Friday but that I should ask her again and give her more notice next time.

Candice's Original AO

He kept asking me out, and I didn't want to hurt his feelings. So finally I told him that I would go out with him, but I didn't really want to. I feel stupid. I should have just said no.

This AO violates all three criteria. It pretty much retells the entire situation, which means that Candice is having a hard time pinpointing thoughts, behaviors, and consequences. Recall that the thoughts and behaviors were already covered in earlier steps. The goal of Step 5 is to help you learn to clearly distinguish among these factors. Identifying certain key words in this AO will help you to generate a good AO. The word *finally* in the second sentence is key to establishing the end parameter and indicates that whatever follows is very close to the end of the situation. In this situation, *finally* pointed to an observable behavior: "I told him that I'd go out with him." You can see that the other information contained in this AO, although important for other areas of the SA (e.g., interpretations and DO), are not needed here.

Candice's Revised AO

I told him that I'd go out with him.

If you have trouble generating good AOs, ask yourself "what would a fly on the wall see at the end of the situation?" and report that.

SUMMARY AND CONCLUSIONS

The process of identifying what you want and what you get is extremely important. We hope this section has helped you to recognize that clearly defining your DO and AO is the first step to closing the gap between them. As you become more skillful in SA, you might realize that the effectiveness of the process in general is heavily dependent on how well you can define the DO and AO. Why? There are many reasons, but most important is that precise, behaviorally defined DOs and AOs allow you to recognize the nature and size of the discrepancy between what you got and what you wanted. Vaguely or otherwise poorly constructed outcomes in Steps 4 and 5 will make fine tuning your behavior much more difficult, and you will find the gap closing much more slowly. Remember, you are the architect of your own recovery. Your skillfulness and dedication will play a large role in the speed and permanence of healing. If you follow the rules outlined here, soon your DO will be your AO.

Chapter 6

Remediation of Interpretations*

This chapter will give you a clear, step-by-step explanation of the process of *remediation of interpretations.* Remediation of interpretations is the process that you go through to change your thoughts and interpretations of events that you experience. Many times, these thoughts and interpretations contribute to a stressful and undesirable outcome. This chapter will outline the process of changing these unhelpful thoughts and interpretations into ones that are more accurate and beneficial and contribute to an outcome that you desire.

Remember, this remediation phase occurs after you complete the five steps of Situational Analysis (SA): (1) describing the event, (2) identify interpretations, (3) identify behaviors, (4) identify your desired outcome (DO), and (5) identify the actual outcome (AO). This chapter explains the therapeutic benefits of remediation of interpretations as a separate, independent process and illustrates the benefits of this process within the context of SA. The case example of Andy and Beth used in previous chapters will illustrate the process of remediation of interpretations, and other examples will provide a context in which to discuss typical obstacles encountered and tips for generating alternative interpretations that you can believe in and act on.

*The primary authors contributing to this chapter were Foluso M. Williams and Rita L. Ketterman.

WHAT HAPPENS AT THIS STEP?

Put simply, interpretation remediation is changing the way you think about and interpret events. One could argue that one of the most difficult aspects of SA is the remediation of interpretations. This is not surprising, especially because thinking is such an automatic process; thus, deliberately changing your thoughts can be challenging. However, in this chapter the process is described in a clear, step-by-step process. Also, the more you practice changing your interpretations, the more automatic the process will become. Constructing interpretations that help you achieve your DO will eventually become second nature.

The remediation of interpretations is an organized, systematic way of examining every interpretation you had in the situation you described in Step 1. You will carefully consider every interpretation you identified at Step 2 and decide whether each one helped you or hindered you on achieving the DO you identified at Step 4. You then will go through the process of reconstructing the interpretations that did not help you in achieving your DO and you will replace those hurtful interpretations with helpful thoughts that would have encouraged the behavior necessary to increase the likelihood of obtaining your DO.

WHY REMEDIATE INTERPRETATIONS?

Looking at the usefulness of your thoughts may seem like a lame attempt to solve some of life's really big problems, but it is, by itself, a very powerful tool. It is amazing what creatures of habit we are, especially in how we think about life circumstances. In Step 2, you learned that your interpretations of events are not always as accurate as you think. You also learned that your perceptions of events and their causes are not always objective; they can be influenced by a variety of personal factors. In addition, you learned that alternative points of view are always possible. In remediation of interpretations, you go beyond awareness of your interpretations to *examine* whether these thoughts are *useful* in the particular situation you've selected to analyze. Although it is not important to label the thought as good or bad, deciding whether or not it is *helpful* in getting what you want forces you to examine whether *how* you interpret the situation is consistent with your goals and desires for that situation. Looking at the utility of your interpretations helps you identify and clarify where it is you want to go and what you want to do. This helps you bring to the forefront of your mind what is most important to you, not only in the moment, but also in the long term.

The simple act of examining your interpretations of events and modifying them so they are in line with your goals prevents the age-old pattern of doing the opposite of what you intended to do. How many times have you said to yourself "I promised myself I wouldn't blow up," or "I really didn't want to eat that," or "I wanted to go to the gym today"? Sometimes, we construct problematic interpretations that may directly or indirectly result in the very outcome that we did not desire.

Examining your thoughts, then, makes you aware of what you *really* want to do rather than just reacting out of habit or impulse. Furthermore, when you recognize that a thought is not useful in a given situation, attempting to think differently can make you aware of the rut your thinking may be in. At times, our thoughts and interpretations actually present us with some limits. The process of SA will make you aware of these limits and will give you the power to change the way you think. This may be an ability that you did not think you had, but by practicing the principles of SA, this ability will become more apparent.

Thought examination also helps you regulate your emotions. Have you ever been so angry, nervous, or afraid that you couldn't think straight? For some of us, emotions rule how we think, and therefore how we act. Oftentimes, emotional responses are the basis for behavior that is regrettable for any number of reasons, from flat-out embarrassment to loss of companionship. For example, how many times have you blown up at somebody you cared about and said some things that you later regretted? Have you ever tried to explain to a friend how he or she had hurt you and observed the situation between the two of you became worse instead of better, simply because you were reacting out of the pain you felt? Watching and analyzing your thoughts for their helpfulness moves you out of emotional thought processes and into rational thought processes. For example, by carefully examining your interpretations, you can calmly and politely explain to your friend why you were hurt instead of jumping to conclusions and acting in ways that can only make a stressful situation worse.

Furthermore, as we discussed in chapter 3, when you start to observe and then change your thoughts, you will often find that your feelings will change naturally, and quite quickly. The link between what you think and how you feel is pretty direct. When the new thoughts you choose are rooted in your desires and goals, the feelings that are connected with them are often both more positive and powerful. Rather than looking for that quick fix for a bad mood by kicking the dog, picking on your spouse, going shopping, getting drunk, or eating a gallon of ice cream, identifying and modifying your thoughts about a situation can help you find ways to reach your goals and to stabilize or improve your mood.

Remediation of thoughts becomes even more powerful when considered in the context of the rest of SA. As you change your thoughts, it is far easier to imagine changing your behavior. What once seemed impossible becomes plausible. In addition, changing thoughts and subsequent behavior can greatly increase your chances of reaching your DOs, and it makes the link between your daily thoughts and behaviors and your short- and long-term goals more concrete. When you begin to experience this process, you will find that your interpretations and resulting behaviors will be fashioned in a direct and purposeful way.

Changing the way you think is helpful within the context of SA for a variety of reasons. The way you think and act has a direct effect on what happens in situations. By assessing whether a thought helps you achieve what you want out of a situation, you begin to train yourself to think in a more beneficial way. Remember, this is a process—your interpretations will not change overnight. However, with training and practice, you will begin to generate interpretations that are powerful tools to help you achieve your DOs in stressful situations. We have provided a worksheet to help you as you learn this step (see Fig. 6.1). In SA, the situations that you analyze are brief and concrete slices of time rather than big events that have taken place over a long period of time. When you use these slices of time as a context in which to examine and change your interpretations, the skills you learn will have a domino effect to other circumstances and events that you experience in life. Changing the way you think in a situation will benefit you not only when you experience that situation itself, but also when you come across other situations and circumstances in your life.

ANDY AND BETH'S SITUATION

Recall that Andy's goal in therapy was to learn to communicate more productively with his fiancée, Beth, and to find a way to mend their relationship. At this point, Andy has already accomplished several steps in the process of SA. He has specified the situational slice of time and has identified all his interpretations and behaviors in the situation. In addition, he has constructed his AO and DO. Now, Andy has reached the remediation phase of SA, in which he will review his interpretations, decide whether they helped or hurt him, and then revise them accordingly.

Worksheet for Revising Your Interpretations

Step 1: Write down all your interpretations.

1. ____
2. ____
3. ____
4. ____

Step 2: Write down your desired outcome.

My desired outcome for the situation was ____________________

____

Step 3: Examine each interpretation: Did it HELP or HURT in getting your desired outcome?

Circle:

1: HELPED or HURT
2: HELPED or HURT
3: HELPED or HURT
4: HELPED or HURT

Step 4: Focus on the interpretations that HURT and begin to CHANGE them.

Was your interpretation. . . . . .

1. Too extreme? (She NEVER listens to how I feel!)
2. Based on emotion? (I felt rejected, that means that I am a loser.)
3. Based on assumptions? (He should have known that I would not like that!)
4. Unrealistic? No evidence to back it up? (I know he thinks that I am lazy.)
5. Look for words such as "can't" "never" and "always".

Step 5: Tips on changing your interpretations:

1. Look for alternative possibilities.
2. Remember feelings don't always equal reality.
3. Make sure it is accurate: Look for evidence.

Step 6: Keeping these tips in mind, revise your interpretations.

1. ____
2. ____
3. ____
4. ____

Step 7: Ask these questions about each of your new interpretations:

1. Does it help me achieve my desired outcome?
2. Is it based on reality, and not my emotion?
3. Is it free of extremes? (can't, never, always)

FIG. 6.1. Worksheet for revising your interpretations. Figure created by Foluso M. Williams and Rita L. Ketterman.

Interpretations

1. Beth should have known that I would want her to invite me along.
2. I'm not going to tell her that I'm upset, because she will just get angry.
3. She'd rather hang out with her friends than me, like she doesn't even like me anymore.

Desired Outcome

Andy identified his DO: "I wanted to stand up for myself by telling her I felt rejected and lonely when she left me out of her plans tonight."

Andy's situation is a pretty common one. How he feels is understandable, given the circumstances. However, as you have seen, the situation ended with an outcome that was not desired. How did this happen? Let's examine Andy's interpretations and see how they might have contributed to the stressful outcome by examining a conversation between the therapist and Andy.

Therapist (T): So, Andy, let's go over your SA worksheet.

Andy (A): OK.

T: Do you remember what goes on in the remediation of interpretations?

A: Yeah; that's when I have to go through all of my interpretations and see whether they helped me or hurt me in getting what I wanted.

T: That's right. So, before we begin, remember that everything is anchored to your DO. Let's examine it before we go on. Remember, you made a couple of changes to it when we went through Step 4.

A: My DO was to stand up for myself by telling her I felt rejected and lonely when she left me out of her plans.

T: Great! Let's go through your interpretations. How about the first one?

A: (*reading*) "Beth should have known that I wanted to come along."

T: Did that help you or hurt you in getting what you wanted?

A: Umm, well, it didn't help.

T: Why?

A: Not sure, really. I just know it made me feel upset, and I reacted to her negatively because of that. But I still think she should have known!

T: OK. Let's examine that statement. "Beth should have known that I wanted to come along." Well, based on this statement, you must have told her you wanted to come along, right?

A: Ummm, well actually, I didn't.

T: Well, then how should she have known?

A: She's my fiancée; she is supposed to know that stuff!

T: Let's look at the accuracy of this statement. Do you think its realistic to assume somebody should know something you haven't expressed to them?

A: No.

T: So, how can we change this into an interpretation that might have helped you achieve your DO?

A: Well, since it was not accurate, I guess I can start by making it more accurate. Since I didn't tell her how I felt, there is a possibility that she did not know how I felt.

T: That's great, Andy. Did you see that? You just generated another interpretation.

A: Yeah, and I think it would help me in getting what I wanted. By understanding that she might not have known how I felt, I would not have acted toward her the way I did. I would have been able to tell her how I felt, without accusing her of having to know better.

T: Good job, Andy. When you have an interpretation that does not help you get what you want, you can try a couple of things to help you come up with a better interpretation. For example, you can start out by examining how accurate your interpretation is, or you can try looking for other explanations. Let's move on to the next interpretation on your list.

A: OK. (*reading*) "I'm not going to tell her that I am upset, because she will just get angry."

T: Did that help you or hurt you in getting what you wanted?

A: Didn't help for sure, because she got angry anyway!

T: You're right. Why else didn't that interpretation help?

A: Well, I don't know. I mean, Beth does get angry when I tell her I am upset. This happens a lot.

T: It's understandable why you feel that way. It can be a stressful experience to tell people how we feel sometimes, especially when they react in ways we don't like.

A: Yeah, that's how I feel.

T: Well, let's look at that statement for a second. Let's see why having that interpretation did not help you get your DO.

A: Hmm, well, by thinking that way, I didn't end up telling her that I felt upset. So, instead of telling her how I felt, I assumed she'd get upset and I just pouted instead.

T: The fact is, Beth may or may not get upset. But you won't know unless you tell her how you feel.

A: That's true.

T: OK. So how do we change that to help you get what you want?

A: She needs to know how I feel about this. Keeping my feelings to myself out of fear of how she will react doesn't help anything.

T: All right! So how does having this new interpretation help you get what you want?

A: Realizing that she needs to know how I feel helps me to put things in the right perspective. Before we can start the process of communication, Beth needs to know how I feel. Her getting upset is not worth the price of hiding my feelings from her and reacting in a way that makes the situation worse.

T: Great job, Andy. Let's look at your last interpretation. Can you read that for me?

A: Sure. (*reading*) "She'd rather hang out with her friends than me, like she doesn't even like me anymore."

T: Did this help or hurt you in getting your DO?

A: It hurt.

T: Why?

A: Because by thinking this way, I had all these feelings of hurt and anger brewing inside me. And that affected the way I reacted to her. It would be more difficult to calmly and clearly express how I felt to her, if I was thinking that she didn't like me anymore.

T: That is true.

A: But I don't know what to think. I mean, she didn't even ask if I wanted to come! She just booked out. If she cared about me and liked hanging out with me, she would have asked me to come along.

T: Well, I can see how you feel that way, Andy. It hurts when you feel like you have been left out. But just because you feel that way, does that mean that is necessarily the truth?

A: Well—no.

T: That's right. The way you feel about a situation does not always reflect the truth of the situation.

A: I'm stuck. I'm not sure how to come up with another interpretation.

T: OK. What can we use when we are stuck?

A: Well, I can look at how accurate this is, and maybe consider some alternatives.

T: OK.

A: I mean, I don't hang out with Beth 24-7. I do things with others, and it doesn't mean I don't like her. So, I guess it is possible for Beth to like spending time with me and still hang out with other people.

T: You've made a good point there, Andy. I like the fact that you are being more flexible. You were able to find a different explanation for Beth's behavior. You realize that liking someone does not exclude you from spending time with other people.

A: Yeah, that's true. You know, maybe it's not that she doesn't have fun with me, she just wants to spend some time alone with her friends.

T: How does having that interpretation help you with your DO?

A: It definitely helps. By not feeling like I was the victim, it makes it easier for me to explain to her how I feel, in a clear way. It makes it easier not to react out of hurt.

T: Good job, Andy! You're really coming along.

This case example illustrates the process of changing your interpretations. It is easy to understand how Andy came up with his original interpretations about the situation. Many of us think similarly, and at first glance these interpretations seem pretty normal. However, as Andy began to closely examine them, he saw that they did not help him get what he wanted out of the situation. By analyzing *why* the interpretations were not helpful, he was able to come up with interpretations that were more helpful. This is not an easy process, and in the next sections we explore some possible obstacles in this process and offer tips to help you.

COMMON STUMBLING BLOCKS IN THE REMEDIATION OF INTERPRETATIONS

If changing your thoughts were easy, this workbook would not need to be written. The truth is that although your thoughts may not be helpful in some ways, they likely have other benefits. The following are some common obstacles to the remediation of interpretations:

- Getting past the old thoughts
- Getting stuck in the emotion
- Liking your old thoughts
- Being afraid to think differently
- Blaming other people, places, and things
- Taking on more than your share of the responsibility

The identification of both the pros and the cons connected with a particular train of thought may help you to further assess whether the thought is helpful or hurtful in achieving your DO. The question is, "What is the payoff of this interpretation?" Don't despair, however: If you can't figure this out, you can trust the process of SA to demonstrate why you might be hanging onto old thought patterns. Here are some tips for generating alternative interpretations:

- *Consider the opposite.* Every concept has a polar opposite (e.g., dark and light, fat and thin, old and new). Considering the polar opposite of what we are thinking can help us to see another point of view. Both can be tested against reality to see which has greater veracity and/or utility in the specific situation.
- *Become a witness: Watch what is occurring as if you were watching a play.* If you tend to react emotionally before thinking, this technique is for you! By imagining yourself watching events as if they were a play, you take the role of the audience, which separates you from the action. This helps you to practice emotional detachment and, rather than getting caught up in the feelings, you can rationally process what is happening, which helps you choose your thoughts and behavior.
- *Keep in mind what you really want to achieve.* This sounds obvious, but because human beings like to get immediate reinforcement, short-term needs often force long-term goals into the background. Again, the key is to get away from the *emotional* desire for instant gratification (whether it be food, sex, material goods, or the desire to take out your frustration on others) and connect with the more rational, long-term goal. This will help you determine if what you are thinking is helpful or harmful to what is important in the long run.
- *Think of what you might tell your best friend in the same situation.* You might be your own worst critic: Although you may not be able to find compassion for yourself, ironically, you may be wonderfully supportive to others. If you can't find compassion for yourself, imagine that you are advising a good friend with the same problem. What would you say to help support him or her?
- *What would someone you admire or respect say?* If you tend to not trust your own judgment, at least in some areas of life, perhaps there is someone whom you respect who might be able to inject some objectivity to the situation—for example, a parent, sibling, teacher, coworker, supervisor, your own children, spiritual or religious advisor, or counselor.
- *What's the evidence? How do you know what you know? What are alternative explanations?* These questions help you to look at the current facts of the situation to gauge the appropriateness of your response. Sometimes your emotional reaction is not based on current events but is tied to painful or upsetting historical events that may have some similarity.

• *Overstate or exaggerate the thought: Look for humor or absurdity.* If you tend to blow things out of proportion, the remedy is to continue to do so until the whole scenario explodes! When you deliberately exaggerate the situation and its consequences, you will eventually realize that the problem is that you have lost your perspective, and this will help you think about the event in more realistic terms.

• *Write down alternative thoughts, and carry them with you.* Reacting to situations with anxiety, panic, or anger will detract from your ability to think rationally. If none of the other suggestions are helpful, keep an index card with you that lists rational thoughts to help you detach from the emotional content and help you think from an objective point of view.

Now let's take a look at how some people have overcome these obstacles using the preceding tips.

OTHER EXAMPLES

Bill's Situation: Getting Past the Old Thoughts

Bill came into therapy because he didn't have much of a social life and had great difficulty connecting with potential romantic interests. He really wanted to date and have a romantic relationship, but whenever he came into contact with a woman to whom he was attracted, his internal dialogue would begin telling him why she wouldn't be interested in him and why he shouldn't bother. His interpretations typically went something like this:

1. I'm too fat; she'll never be attracted to me.
2. I'm afraid I'll sound or look stupid to her.
3. She probably has a boyfriend already, anyway.

Clearly, these thoughts did not help Bill achieve his DO, but his self-esteem was so low that he had a hard time replacing these old, threadbare thoughts with thoughts that would help him get a date. Examining the evidence enabled Bill to come up with these alternatives:

1. I am not unattractive; even if I am slightly overweight, I have many good features.
2. I get good grades and am not stupid.

3. I know how to break the ice, because I have done it before.
4. I have no idea if she is available . . . if I don't ask, I'll never know!

These thoughts helped Bill approach romantic interests and broaden his social life.

Samantha's Situation: Getting Stuck in the Emotion

Samantha sought help from her therapist when her boyfriend began using crack cocaine after almost a year of abstinence. She was certain that she knew what he needed to do to avoid crack use, and she spent every waking moment trying to help him. She kept his car keys, took his money, locked up his valuables, and called him several times a day on his cell phone. Despite all of her efforts, he would periodically use, which led to financial problems, legal problems, and violent interactions with Samantha. Although her anger was understandable, Samantha was stuck in self-righteous anger and couldn't get past the idea that she was right and he was wrong. Her typical interpretations of his actions were as follows:

1. If he'd only do what I tell him to, he'd get better.
2. Why can't he see what he is doing to me?
3. He is being so stupid! Now I'm going to have to come up with the rent money again!

These thoughts maintained her angry, agitated state and further convinced her that she could make him stop using crack cocaine. Furthermore, her anger fueled confrontations with her boyfriend that often led to physical violence. In this case, Samantha practiced becoming a witness to events so that she could emotionally detach, see that her boyfriend's actions were about his addiction to a powerful drug rather than something he was doing to deliberately hurt her, and observe how her efforts to control his behavior were not helping her achieve her DO. Witnessing events helped Samantha to generate these alternative interpretations:

1. He doesn't know how to handle emotions, so he uses crack instead.
2. Crack is a powerful drug, and he is physically and psychologically addicted.

3. He hurts himself as much as he hurts me.
4. I am the one who is acting crazy, trying to control someone else's behavior. I cannot take responsibility for his life.

These interpretations allowed Samantha to stop reacting to his drug use with anger and begin to take steps to protect herself from his erratic behavior.

Jo's Situation: Liking Your Old Thoughts and Being Afraid to Think Differently

Jo sought help because she felt incompetent, overwhelmed, and unable to delegate duties to the 15 employees she supervised, yet was afraid to ask for help because she believed that she would be letting her supervisor and coworkers down. Her "selflessness" led her to feel like a failure. Jo resisted generating alternative interpretations of her work experience, because she felt that they were unrealistic expectations and that she would be setting herself up for disappointment, which she wanted to avoid at all costs, because she believed she had experienced enough disappointment in her life. These are the thoughts that she was afraid to change:

1. I don't know what I am doing. Every day there is something new to learn.
2. There's no point in asking for help; I won't get it, anyway.
3. If a crisis comes up, I won't know how to handle it.

Jo was good at comforting and supporting others but could not give herself the same type of consideration that she could give others. She was asked to imagine that her best friend had a similar work situation and asked Jo for her input. These are the alternative interpretations that Jo created:

1. Didn't your supervisor ask you to take this position? Surely she must feel you are qualified.
2. If I know you, you are too busy being self-sufficient to ask for help!
3. You are a single parent—of course you know how to handle crises!

Jake's Situation: Blaming Other People, Places, and Things

Jake came into therapy when his three roommates were arrested for dealing and growing marijuana in the home that they shared near the college they attended. Initially, the pot was to be for personal use, but the financial benefits of dealing proved to be too tempting for the starving college students. When the money was coming in, Jake didn't bother to consider that the potential negative consequences of this enterprise might endanger his ability to go to law school. When his roommates were arrested, Jake felt he had the chance to extricate himself from this situation and his roommates as quickly as possible without harm to his reputation, by immediately breaking his lease and moving away. Jake's interpretations clearly laid the blame for the situation at the feet of his roommates. His interpretations were as follows:

1. They were only supposed to grow enough for themselves.
2. They weren't supposed to sell it to anyone but their friends; they got greedy.
3. When we first talked about it, I was against it.

The therapist could see that Jake was ignoring many facts that pointed to his responsibility in creating the problematic situation. First, he had agreed with the growing and selling arrangement, as it saved him money in drug expenditures. He had never complained when he saw more dealing going on than he originally anticipated and was very glad to receive a part of the profits, as it allowed him to go to school full time without having to work as well. Rather than challenging these facts directly, the therapist used deliberate exaggeration of his innocence to make the point that he had more culpability than he wanted to admit. Jake generated the following interpretations:

1. I agreed to allow the marijuana to be grown in the house.
2. I could have asked them to stop dealing, and not taken the money or kept smoking the pot.
3. I knew it was getting out of hand, but I didn't leave because I didn't want to make them suspicious.
4. I am lucky I didn't get caught. I need to talk with the landlord and see if I can get out of my lease.

These thoughts helped Jake realize that honestly addressing the situation rather than blaming others might go much further in achieving his DO, which was to convince his landlord that he needed to get out of his lease so that he could stop this illicit activity and focus on his long-term goal.

Peggy's Situation: Taking on More Than Your Share of the Responsibility

Peggy came to therapy to help her sort out her relationship with her husband. She loved him very much, but she felt inadequate as a wife and mother and like a financial burden since she had stopped working to care for their children several years before. They frequently argued about everyday matters and, over time, these arguments left Peggy feeling confused and inadequate. This particular argument arose one evening when her husband had come home late from work after an especially grueling day. When eating the dinner that Peggy had kept warm for him, her husband went to the pantry to get some bread, but the cupboard was bare. This prompted an angry tirade from her husband about Peggy's failure to take care of these "minor details." This is what her husband's anger meant to Peggy:

1. Since I no longer work, it is my job to make sure we have what we need.
2. He takes such good care of me, and I can't even keep bread in the pantry.
3. I spend too much time on my gardening and needlework and don't pay attention to my family's needs.

What is obvious to you and us, but not to Peggy, was the self-beating nature of these thoughts maintained her confusion and sense of inadequacy. Peggy was asked to replay the scene in her mind but to watch it as if it were a play. From this vantage point, Peggy could see clearly that her husband was overreacting to a minor problem, probably because he had had a bad day, and that his tirade was not really about her inability to care for her family. Also, she was asked to do some reality testing, and she realized that running out of bread did not make her a bad wife and mother. She was accepting too much responsibility for this argument, because she often felt guilty about not contributing financially to the household. Here are Peggy's revised interpretations:

1. He's tired and frustrated about other things; he really isn't angry about the bread.
2. I'm not the only one who can go to the grocery store!
3. I do plenty of good things to care for my family; I am human and sometimes forget things.

These thoughts helped Peggy realize that her husband had contributed to the argument and that she did not have to take responsibility for his frustration and then mentally beat herself up over it because of a simple oversight. In time, applying these techniques helped to decrease Peggy's confusion and increase her self-esteem.

SUMMARY AND CONCLUSIONS

Remediation of interpretations is a critical component of SA. This process requires you to go through all of your interpretations of a situation and examine what role they played in the achievement of your DO. Analyzing each interpretation to assess whether it hurt you or helped you in getting what you wanted out of a situation is an important process, primarily because identifying why certain interpretations are problematic will help you form better interpretations in future situations. Remember, as arduous as this process may seem, it is helping you change the way you think about and interpret situations. You are changing ways of thinking that lead to stressful outcomes and are adopting new ways of thinking that should greatly increase your chances of getting what you want out of life.

Chapter 7

Behavioral Remediation*

The behavioral remediation phase is closely tied with Step 3 of Situational Analysis (SA) and similar to the interpretation remediation phase described in chapter 6. Recall that in Step 3 you described the specific behaviors you engaged in during the situation you are analyzing. During the behavioral remediation phase you will examine whether and how each of your behaviors (i.e., what you said, how you said it, and your posture and body language during the situation) positively or negatively affected your chances of achieving your desired outcome (DO) for the situation. Then, after you have determined each behavior's utility in this respect, you will think of ways in which you might have replaced hurtful behaviors with helpful ones.

WHAT HAPPENS IN BEHAVIORAL REMEDIATION?

The first goal of this step is to determine if the way you behaved during the slice of time detailed in Step 1 (situational description) positively or negatively affected your chances of achieving your DO for the situation. How exactly is this accomplished? First, you and your therapist will examine each of the behaviors you described at Step 3 of the SA worksheet in turn. Then you

*The primary authors contributing to this chapter were Leonardo Bobadilla and Justin D. Michels.

will determine how useful each of your behaviors was, by evaluating whether each one was *helpful* or *hurtful* to attaining your DO. It is important to analyze each behavior on an individual basis, because every single behavior enacted during the situation contributes to your ability to obtain (or not obtain) your DO. Thus, during the behavioral remediation phase of SA you will read each of the behaviors you recorded on the SA worksheet and, immediately after you finish reviewing a behavior, you will ask yourself whether that behavior helped or hurt you in obtaining your DO.

In other words, you will closely examine each of the things that you said, how you said them, how you acted, and what your body language communicated during the situation, and determine whether they respectively helped or hurt your chances of getting what you wanted out of the situation. Initially, you may find making the decision about how useful your behaviors were to be difficult, because some of these behaviors may be the usual way in which you react or express yourself (we address more of the difficulties associated with this phase later). This difficulty is a very common one among people who are first learning to use SA. You may want to think of the first few times you use SA as training experiences. During this initial training, you may ask your therapist for help in deciding whether your behaviors were useful. Others (e.g., supportive friends, a therapist) can provide a valuable third-person perspective on your behaviors and can initially provide suggestions to help you decide how useful your behaviors were in a given situation. However, as you progress and become more familiar with the process of SA, you will be able to determine more easily the utility of your behaviors during everyday situations.

As you may have guessed, the ultimate goal of this phase is to determine what kinds of behaviors got in the way of obtaining your DO, so that you can start to understand where changes could be made. Once you have determined that a behavior was hurtful, the next task is to figure out a way in which, if you had the situation to do all over again, you might replace this hurtful behavior with a helpful one. During the process of replacing hurtful behaviors with helpful ones, it is of the utmost importance that you keep in mind that the new, helpful behaviors you come up with pertain to *your* behavior (as opposed to that of someone else in the situation) and are anchored to the realistic, attainable DO you described in Step 4. People who are first learning to use SA commonly think of new behaviors in the remediation phase that are not directly related to the described DO or that are centered around another person's behavior. We'll discuss these types of mistakes further, and give examples later in this chapter. For now, simply remember that this pitfall is easily overcome with practice.

WHY REMEDIATE BEHAVIORS?

Within the context of SA, the main therapeutic effect of this step comes from two sources. The first relates to the immediate insight you obtain regarding the effect that your actions have on your DOs and on other persons with whom you interact. By examining each behavior individually and determining its utility, you will be able to see that the tone of voice you use to say something, or the manner in which you use your body language to express yourself, sends a message to other people that directly affects the outcome of the situation. The second therapeutic effect of this step within the context of SA is related to the realization that it is possible for you to generate alternative behaviors that will better allow you to obtain your DOs. These two therapeutic effects provide what is perhaps one of the most important messages of SA: Stressful situations usually do not just randomly happen to people; to a great extent, you have a direct role in creating either beneficial or detrimental outcomes for yourself in these situations.

As mentioned before, some of the difficulty associated with this step is the fact that some of the behaviors you will be remediating may be the usual ways you act or respond during difficult circumstances. This is precisely the main reason why the behavioral remediation step is therapeutic, even on its own. You may find, for example, that during arguments you have a tendency to first raise your voice, then talk very fast without listening to what the other person has to say, and finally storm out of the room to cool off. Although this pattern may have some immediate benefits for you (e.g., lets you feel like you had your say and gets you out of the situation before it worsens), the behavioral remediation step will show you that these reactions are often keeping you from obtaining not only your short-term DOs for the situation, but also your longer term goals for your life.

Thus, by examining the situation through the orderly, stepwise structure of SA, you might discover that if you imagine yourself engaging in different behaviors (e.g., instead of raising your voice to express your point of view during an argument, you choose to maintain a normal speaking tone of voice, listen to what the other person has to say, and remain in the room until a mutually beneficial accord is reached) you might increase your chances of obtaining your short-term, situation-limited goal (e.g., speaking your mind and diffusing the situation before it worsens). In addition, as you become more experienced with SA, you will become more aware of your behaviors during other interpersonal interactions, more adept at analyzing whether your behaviors are helping or hurting you, and better at replacing hurtful behaviors with helpful ones on an everyday basis.

ANDY AND BETH'S SITUATION

Recall the earlier discussion of the behaviors Andy listed on his SA worksheet at Step 3:

1. All I said was for her to have fun. I didn't ask her if I could come along.
2. My tone of voice was "defeated." I didn't sound happy with her when she left.
3. I wouldn't look at her or smile. I just ignored her and watched TV.

Let's examine these behaviors, one by one, and generate some remediated (more helpful) behaviors. Remember, for each behavior the question is simply "Did that behavior help or hurt Andy in attaining his DO (which was to tell Beth he felt left out and rejected)?"

The first behavior Andy described on his SA worksheet—telling Beth to "have fun" and little else—is an obvious example of the contrast between Andy's DO (to tell Beth how he felt) and his actual behavior in that situation. In this case, what Andy expressed outwardly was pretty much the complete opposite of what he was feeling. This behavior was therefore clearly hurtful to Andy in obtaining his DO and made it much less likely that that outcome would be achieved. What, then, could he have done to repair this contrast? Perhaps if Andy had instead told Beth that he was feeling upset about something, he would have had better luck at achieving his DO of talking to her about feeling left out and rejected. So, instead of just saying "have fun" and little else, Andy could have said, "I was wondering if I could talk to you about something that's bothering me?" By doing this, Andy would at the very least have unequivocally let Beth know that he wanted to speak to her, thereby increasing the chances of obtaining his DO of discussing his feeling left out.

The second behavior in Andy's Step 3 was a subtler interpersonal cue: a "defeated" tone of voice. For Andy, this was probably an attempt to express his wounded and hurt feelings without explicitly verbalizing them. Beth, however, was likely to interpret such a tone as another example of the "sulking" she so disliked. With this in mind, it's easy to understand how she might have misinterpreted his actual intentions—to convey that he felt hurt and rejected by Beth—as an attempt to sabotage her good time. This behavior, too, then, was hurtful to Andy and interfered with his achievement of his DO. How could he remediate this behavior to make it more helpful? By using a more assertive tone, instead of projecting a "sulking" image, Andy might have greatly improved his chances of reaching his DO. In fact, by combining his remediation of the first behavior (telling Beth that something was bothering him) with the second remediation (using a more assertive tone), Andy might have made great strides toward having the conversation he would have liked in this situation.

Andy's third behavior involved eye contact, posture, and interpersonal engagement: By ignoring Beth, not facing her, and watching TV, he again conveyed a sulking attitude and a lack of desire to really express himself. Considering that his DO was to tell Beth how he was feeling, it is easy to see that these behaviors also hurt his chances of getting what he wanted out of the situation. What could he have done instead? Perhaps if in conjunction with his first two remediated behaviors (telling Beth something was bothering him and using an assertive tone) Andy had also looked at her directly, his DO might have been more easily obtained.

To summarize, let's list the behaviors that Andy displayed during the situation and compare them to the new, remediated behaviors with which he could have replaced them.

Previous Hurtful Behavior	*Remediated Helpful Behavior*
All I said was for her to have fun. I didn't ask her if I could come along.	Told her something was bothering me and I'd like to talk about it.
My tone of voice was "defeated." I didn't sound happy with her when she left.	Used an assertive tone of voice.
I wouldn't look at her or smile. I just ignored her and watched TV.	Looked directly at her when I spoke.
Desired Outcome Achieved: No	Increased Chances of Obtaining Desired Outcome: Definitely

When you are remediating the behaviors from Step 3 on your own, it may be helpful for you to use the worksheet presented in Fig. 7.1, which is designed to help you craft on-target, remediated behaviors in your own SA work.

COMMON STUMBLING BLOCKS

As with the other steps of SA, remediating hurtful/inappropriate behaviors can be difficult. Just as it is sometimes difficult to identify specific problem behaviors in the first place, actually taking action to remediate them may

Worksheet for Behavioral Remediation

1) *Evaluating utility of behaviors.*

   a) Were the behaviors enacted during the situation hurtful? In other words, did what you said, how you said it, how you acted, and what your body language communicated during the situation decrease your chances of obtaining your desired outcome?

   Yes____ No____

If you answered yes, then you probably have enacted a hurtful behavior and it will need to be remediated.

   b) Is the behavior that you enacted during the situation a "usual" way in which you react?

   Yes____ No____

   c) Has this usual way of acting kept you from achieving your desired outcomes in the past?

   Yes____ No____

If you answered yes to BOTH 1b and 1c, then you have likely enacted a hurtful behavior and it will need to be remediated.

2) *Remediating Hurtful Behaviors*

   a) Are the remediated behaviors you have come up with, different "usual" ways in which you react? Has this usual way of acting kept you from achieving your desired outcomes?

   Yes____ No____

If you answered yes to either of these questions then consider revising your behaviors again. You may have supplanted one "old hurtful" way of acting with another "old hurtful" way of acting.

   b) Does the remediated behavior rely on another person changing his or her thoughts and/or behaviors in order for you to obtain your desired outcome?

   Yes____ No____

If you answered yes then consider revising your behaviors again. You have elicited a behavior that is centered on another person's thoughts or behaviors and not your own. Remember you cannot control other persons' thoughts or behaviors.

If you answered NO to all of the above questions, congratulations! You have successfully identified and remediated hurtful behaviors. With practice you will soon be enacting them in everyday situations almost automatically.

FIG. 7.1. Worksheet for Behavioral Remediation. Figure created by Leonardo Bobadilla and Justin D. Michels.

represent a stumbling block. In this section we discuss some common difficulties at this step and potential ways of dealing with them. A common issue associated with remediating problem behaviors is the natural human tendency to fall into automatic patterns of behavior in response to similar situations. In other words, we tend to form habits in our interactions with others, and these can be hard habits to break, especially if we've grown comfortable with these habits over a long period of time. In the case of our main example, Andy may have adopted a defeated tone of voice as a way to indirectly express his unhappiness, even though time and again this behavior fails to help him reach his goals and may instead annoy his girlfriend. Because such behaviors may become so ingrained, remediating them, or even imagining possible means of remediating them, may seem utterly unthinkable at first. If you stick to the step-by-step process of SA, this should be made somewhat easier. Also, once you've mastered the skill of identifying problem behaviors, an objective third party (e.g., a friend, a spouse, a therapist) can often open your eyes to possible courses of action that might not be obvious to you.

As mentioned before, once people are able to identify the hurtful behaviors in a given SA exercise, it is a common mistake to replace them with new behaviors that either are not directly related to the DO described at Step 4 or are centered on another person's behavior. In the case of Andy, for example, he may find himself considering remediated behaviors such as "I wish Beth would not call her friends to go out." Although this remediated behavior may represent an ideal DO for Andy, it is not very helpful in this situation, because it is not centered on his behavior. As you learned in chapter 5, you cannot change the way others act or think.

Enacting remediated behaviors in "real time," as new situations arise, is also commonly cited as a difficulty with SA. It's one thing to write down what you should have done in a situation once it's already over, or to talk with your therapist in an environment without the emotional charge that characterized the original situation. It's another thing entirely to actively force yourself to compare your behaviors to your DO (or even to identify that outcome) in the midst of a real-life conflict. Although there is no quick fix for this problem, rest assured that, with practice, in the form of repeatedly filling out SA forms and discussing them, such in-the-moment remediations will become much more automatic. Remember, the goal is for the entire SA process to become part of your everyday repertoire of interpersonal skills; it is natural and expected that you should need some time and practice to take it all in and make it your own.

OTHER EXAMPLES

To further exemplify the common difficulties (and successes) experienced during this step, we have included additional examples of people remediating their behaviors with the help of their therapists. As you read each example, see if you can identify the "utility" of the behaviors and some of the common mistakes committed by the persons in each example.

Example 1: Sheila

Sheila is a 24-year-old college senior who came to therapy seeking help with dealing with her shyness and her difficulties meeting new people. Although Sheila expressed a desire to be able to relate to and talk to people in social situations, she often found herself paralyzed with fears of rejection. This resulted in a lack of friends and dating partners. The following excerpt is from an exchange with her therapist in which they reviewed Sheila's SA worksheet involving a party she was invited to attend and remediated her behaviors. Her DO was to be able to talk to new people at the party and perhaps exchange phone numbers with a new acquaintance. Let's look at some of the behaviors she identified in Step 3 of her SA worksheet:

1. I arrived at the party and stood in the corner waiting for someone to talk to me.
2. I stood against the wall, holding my soda, listening to the music. I did not move the whole time and avoided eye contact with people.
3. After 30 minutes I left without talking to anybody or looking for my friend who was hosting the party.

The following is a transcript of the behavioral remediation process Sheila underwent with her therapist:

Therapist (T): OK, Sheila, let's start with the first behavior: standing in the corner and waiting for someone to talk to you. Did that help you or hurt you in achieving your DO?

Sheila (S): I don't know. Usually when I go to a party, I just wait for people to come talk to me, and that's how I usually meet people.

T: What was your DO for this situation?

S: To be able to talk to new people and maybe exchange phone numbers with somebody.

T: And what actually happened?

S: I left without talking to anybody.

T: So, keeping in mind your DO and what actually happened, do you think that standing in the corner helped or hurt you?

S: Well, I guess it hurt now that you put it that way . . .

T: Yes, it seems like it may have hurt. So, what helpful behavior could you have replaced it with? What behavior might have helped you achieve your DO?

S: Maybe if I had started a short conversation with someone when I got my drink . . . that may have helped.

T: You may be right; that might have helped break the ice and helped you meet someone.

Sheila's example demonstrates how your usual ways of reacting, though they may feel natural or comfortable for you, are not always helpful when it comes to achieving your DOs for specific situations.

Example 2: Adrian

In this example, Adrian, a 29-year-old engineer who came to therapy seeking help with anger management, has already identified hurtful behaviors and is now generating alternative helpful behaviors. In this situation, Adrian's DO was to be able to tell his girlfriend that he was tired and needed to relax before having to deal with household problems. Instead, he became agitated when she asked what was wrong, and they ended up yelling at each other.

Adrian's first behavior in Step 3 was the following: "I got home, slammed the door closed, dropped my suitcase by the door, and went to the living room, where my girlfriend was watching TV."

During the remediation phase, Adrian identified this behavior as a hurtful one. In the following transcript, Adrian attempts to remediate this behavior with the aid of his therapist.

Therapist (T): OK, Adrian, if this was a hurtful behavior, what helpful behavior could you have replaced it with?

Adrian (A): Well, instead of slamming the door I could have closed it normally, and I could have just set my suitcase on the floor instead of dropping it so that I would not get even more worked up about the hell of a day I had.

T: You may be right Adrian—maybe doing those things only made you feel more worked up. Good job. Let's move on to the next behavior.

Adrian's second behavior as identified in Step 3 of SA was the following: "Sat down in front of the TV without saying anything, grabbed the remote control, and started changing the channels as I sighed loudly."

Adrian had previously identified this as a hurtful behavior with respect to obtaining his DO of telling his girlfriend he was tired and needed to relax.

Therapist (T): So, if those behaviors hurt, what could you have done instead to achieve your DO?

Adrian (A): Well, I could have at least said "hello" to her, and then instead of just grabbing the remote control, I could have asked her if I could change the channel.

T: I agree with you, Adrian—I think that doing those things may have really helped you achieve your DO. Let's examine the third behavior.

Adrian's third behavior as identified in Step 3 of SA was the following: "I became irritated when she asked me what was wrong, and I asked her if she was blind and could not see that I was tired."

Adrian had previously determined that this was also a hurtful in obtaining his DO of telling his girlfriend that he was tired and needed to relax.

Therapist (T): OK, Adrian, what could you have done on this one?

Adrian (A): Well, see, on this one I know the behavior is hurtful, but I really think that she should have by now figured out what was wrong with me.

T: I see; so what you are saying is that it should have been obvious to her how you were feeling?

A: Exactly. She's not stupid; there have been plenty of times I've come home like that and it was obvious that I was tired.

T: But, in this situation Adrian, without considering past times, did she have to know how you were feeling?

A: Well, even without thinking about other times, if I saw her coming into the house, plopping on the couch and sighing loudly, I would have easily figured out what was up.

T: Could there be any other reason for anybody to act like that when they come home?

A: I suppose so . . . I guess if they were mad because somebody cut them off in traffic or something.

T: So, is it possible that because of the way you were acting, she might have thought something else was the matter with you?

A: I guess so . . .

T: And did you have control over what she thought was wrong with you?

A: Well, no, I can't control what she thinks.

T: Exactly, Adrian. Very good. You can't control her thoughts, so you may think your body language says one thing but other people think something completely different. So what could you have done to achieve your DO?

A: Well, I could've just told her I had a long day and needed to unwind for a little bit.

In this example, Adrian was able to easily remediate most of his behaviors. However, the remediation of the last behavior listed in Step 3 was a bit more difficult for him, because his focus was on his girlfriend's behavior and what she should have observed. Thus, he was not making progress in finding a helpful remediated behavior. Only by changing the focus back to his own behavior could Adrian find an alternative behavior more likely to help him achieve his DO.

SUMMARY AND CONCLUSIONS

The behavioral remediation step is not only a crucial part of the process of SA; it also has therapeutic benefits all by itself. These benefits arise from the fact that it forces you to objectively and carefully review the influence of behaviors of yours that you may not recognize as problematic. Indeed, these types of behaviors may have become a common way for you to act or react to others, particularly during stressful situations, and they may thus seem so automatic to you that you forget that you have control over them or that they may be interfering with your personal goals. Because you are likely to be accustomed to these patterns of behavior, you may experience some difficulty in deciding whether they were helpful or hurtful to you in the context of a given situation; however, with practice and with your therapist's help you will soon find that this process of evaluation, and the generation of alternative, more helpful behaviors, becomes much easier. As always, of course, the ultimate goal is to develop these skills to the point that you are able to apply the principles from this step in your everyday living, so that in the midst of a stressful situation you can think about your DO and direct your behavior accordingly. When you reach that point, you'll be amazed how much more smoothly these situations seem to go!

Chapter 8

Concluding Remarks*

We all have problems in our lives. Perhaps you have difficulty getting along with others in social situations or at work. Perhaps you have communication problems in your marriage, or difficulty managing your children. Perhaps you struggle with anger control, or suffer from anxiety or depression. The difficulty with problems such as these is often that they are so broad, so all encompassing, and are wreaking such havoc on your daily life and functioning, that it is hard to know where to begin to address them or strive for change. However, the view we have attempted to convey throughout this workbook is that whatever the problems you face, certain commonalities are very likely to apply. The general problems you experience are manifested in multiple discrete, time-limited situations. The outcomes of those situations are influenced by your interpretations and behaviors within those situations. Having realistic and attainable goals for the situations in which you find yourself, and mindfully tailoring your thoughts and behaviors toward those goals, dramatically improves your chances of having situations turn out favorably for you.

This workbook has presented to you the steps of Situational Analysis (SA), a system designed to help you learn to more effectively navigate the events that life throws your way. By becoming more adept at stepping back from specific situations, identifying and modifying your thoughts and be-

*The primary authors contributing to this chapter were Andrea B. Burns, Lorraine R. Reitzel, and Thomas E. Joiner Jr.

haviors, and determining realistic goals for yourself, it is our goal that you should, in time, notice that the improvements you are experiencing in these discrete encounters are generalizing to the "bigger picture" improvements in your life that you truly care about. In other words, the process of SA is intended to provide you with a straightforward method for tackling the huge problems of life one little situation at a time.

REVIEW OF SITUATIONAL ANALYSIS

Each chapter of this workbook has been devoted toward explicating one step of SA. Now that you have had a chance to delve deeply into each one, take a moment to step back and recall the overall process.

At Step 1, you describe a significant situation that occurred in a relatively brief slice of time. Taking a fly on the wall perspective, you outline the highlights of what happened, making sure your story has a beginning, middle, and end.

At Step 2, you identify your interpretations of the situation. What was your personal read of what happened? What did you make of it? What did it mean to you? Specify three to four interpretations, taking care that they reflect thoughts, as opposed to emotions.

At Step 3, you identify your behaviors in the situation. What did you do and say, and how did you do and say it? Consider your tone of voice, pace of speech, eye contact, facial expressions, and body language, as well as your actual words and actions.

At Step 4, you identify your desired outcome (DO) for the situation. If you could wave that magic wand (with its limited powers), how would you have wanted the situation to turn out? Keep the SUPERB principles in mind as you determine a DO that would have been realistic and attainable.

At Step 5, you identify the actual outcome (AO) of the situation. How did the situation you've described turn out in the end? To the extent possible, try to express the AO in behavioral, not emotional terms.

Step 5 marks the end of the first phase of SA. Having thus outlined these elements of a significant situation that has taken place, your remaining task is to analyze the impact your interpretations and behaviors had on your chances of reaching your DO. First, you will review your interpretations, questioning for each whether it helped you or hurt you in getting the outcome you would have preferred. If it helped, great! Make note of that for use in future situations. If it hurt, think of how you might have interpreted that situation in a more helpful manner. Once you've got a handle on a more helpful set of interpretations, you will review and revise your behaviors in the same way.

At first, this process may seem terribly painstaking, requiring a great deal of time and effort considering you're talking about situations that have already passed. However, as you begin to master the process of SA you should begin to notice patterns that seem to be consistently interfering with your attainment of your DOs. Perhaps your interpretations tend to be overly negative or unrealistically pessimistic. Perhaps your thoughts are helpful, but your behaviors are conveying signals that are being perceived the wrong way by others. Perhaps your goals are unrealistic, or too dependent on the actions of others. Whatever your specific pattern, this process will help you to see it and will give you a framework for generating alternative possibilities that will improve your chances of meeting your personal objectives.

OUR CASE EXAMPLE: ANDY AND BETH

The case of Andy and Beth has been presented throughout this workbook to illustrate how SA might be implemented to address pervasive relationship problems by focusing on situational examples of those difficulties. It is important to recognize that the one SA worksheet of Andy's presented in this workbook (Fig. 1.3) would not be sufficient to eliminate Andy and Beth's relationship problems altogether. However, having completed this exercise, Andy might take note of how his thoughts and behaviors in the situation he chose bear a resemblance to his thoughts and actions in other, similar encounters with Beth. By recognizing the manner in which some of his thoughts and actions actually moved him away from his goals with Beth, he can be more wary of such things in the future. If he should continue to subject his stressful encounters with Beth to SA, over time he should learn to consistently resist his unproductive cognitions and actions and instead mindfully focus on more helpful ones.

Let's review the SA worksheet completed by Andy. It initially looked like the SA worksheet in Fig. 8.1. As was noted throughout the chapters of this workbook, there were several problems with Andy's worksheet at the outset. After making key corrections to his situational description, the AO, and his DO, Andy's worksheet looked like the SA worksheet in Fig. 8.2.

Finally, Andy went through the remediation stage of SA, in which he reviewed his interpretations and his behaviors and assessed whether each was helping or hurting him with attaining his DO. In doing so, he realized

Situational Analysis Worksheet 1

Name: *Andy*

Date of Situational Event: *March 4, 2004*

Situational Area: ______ Family ______ Work/School __✓__ Social

---

Instructions: Select a stressful situation that has occurred in your life during the previous week. Please describe the situation using the steps indicated below.

---

1. Describe what happened:
   Beth went out again with her friends on Friday night. They were going to a club to dance and drink. She did not invite me to join them, but rather, passively suggested that I hook up with some of my friends for a "boys' night out." I told her to have a good time. She got all dressed up, kissed me on the cheek, and left. I stayed home and watched TV. She got home at 2:30 in the morning, happy and tired. She didn't even ask me how my night went.

2. Describe your interpretation(s) of what happened:
   1. *Beth should have known that I would want her to invite me along.*
   2. *I'm not going to tell her that I'm upset because she'll just get angry.*
   3. *She'd rather hang out with her friends than me, like she doesn't even like me any more.*
   4. *She doesn't even care that I spent the whole night by myself—again.*

3. Describe what you did during the situation:
   1. *All I said was for her to have fun. I didn't ask if I could come along.*
   2. *Tone of voice: "defeated". I didn't sound happy when she left.*
   3. *I wouldn't look at her or smile. I just ignored her and watched TV.*
   4. *When she came home, I was very quiet and didn't respond when she told me how much fun she'd had.*

4. Describe how you wanted the event to come out for you (Desired Outcome):
   I wanted her to want me to come along. I wanted her to realize that she's being rude by leaving me out and making me feel rejected.

5. Describe how the event came out for you (Actual Outcome):
   We got into an argument when she got home. She told me I made her feel guilty by "pouting" and said that she just needed some space to be on her own. I just let it go and went to sleep on the couch, but I felt awful. She just seemed agitated with me.

RATE: Did you get what you wanted? Yes____ No *X*

FIG. 8.1. Situational Analysis Worksheet 1. Figure adapted from McCullough (2000) by Andrea B. Burns, Lorraine R. Reitzel, and Thomas E. Joiner Jr.

Situational Analysis Worksheet 2

Name: *Andy*

Date of Situational Event: *March 4, 2004*

Situational Area: _______ Family _______ Work/School ___✓___ Social

Instructions: Select a stressful situation that has occurred in your life during the previous week. Please describe the situation using the steps indicated below.

1. Describe what happened:
   Beth told me that she was going to a club with her friends to dance and drink. She did not invite me to join them, but suggested that I hook up with some of my friends for a "boys' night out." I told her to have a good time.

2. Describe your interpretation(s) of what happened:
   1. *Beth should know that I would want her to invite me along.*
   2. *I'm not going to tell her that I'm upset because she'll just get angry.*
   3. *She'd rather hang out with her friends than me, like she doesn't even like me any more.*

3. Describe what you did during the situation:
   1. *All I said was for her to have fun. I didn't ask if I could come along.*
   2. *Tone of voice: "defeated". I didn't sound happy when she left.*
   3. *I wouldn't look at her or smile. I just ignored her and watched TV.*

4. Describe how you wanted the event to come out for you (Desired Outcome):
   I wanted to stand up for myself by telling her I felt rejected and lonely when she left me out of her plans tonight.

5. Describe how the event came out for you (Actual Outcome):
   I stayed at home alone while Beth went out. I felt miserable.

RATE: Did you get what you wanted? Yes _____ No __*X*__

FIG. 8.2. Situational Analysis Worksheet 2. Figure adapted from McCullough (2000) by Andrea B. Burns, Lorraine R. Reitzel, and Thomas E. Joiner Jr.

that most of his thoughts and actions were actually making it less likely that he would get what he wanted from this situation, and with some help he was able to conceive of alternative thoughts and behaviors that might have been more helpful. Having completed the remediation process, his final worksheet looked like the SA worksheet in Fig. 8.3. You can see, as Andy did, what a difference interpretations and behaviors can make!

SITUATIONAL ANALYSIS FOR DIFFERENT PROBLEM AREAS

By this point you should have a good understanding of how SA works. You have learned how each step of the process should proceed, and what common mistakes to avoid, by following the example of Andy and Beth's relationship problems. However, although the case example in this book focuses on a couple having communication problems, there is no reason to assume that this is the only problem with which SA can be useful. In fact, that is one of the best things about SA: It can be applied to many different situations, types of people, and types of problems. SA is such a flexible technique because it works with your unique problems and situations and allows you to specify your own DO, rather than telling you what you ought to want in a situation. SA also helps you think about your interpersonal interactions in a new way—a way that trains you to focus on your thoughts and behaviors in a situation and the effect that they have on how things turn out for you. Finally, SA gives you the control to decide how you want to change, and allows you to see how changing how you think and act in a situation can influence the way things work out for you.

Let's consider how SA can be helpful to people with different types of problems. People suffering from problems with anxiety, including a fear of a specific situation (e.g., talking in public), generalized worry, or out-of-the-blue anxiety attacks, may find SA helpful because it helps them to notice how their thoughts and behaviors contribute to the perpetuation of their anxiety. For example, people who are afraid of talking in public might have thoughts such as "I can't do this," "I'll make a fool of myself," and/or "They'll laugh at me." Therefore, they may engage in the behavior of avoidance (making excuses why they cannot speak in public or otherwise getting out of doing it). This helps to fuel the original fear, which leads into a never-ending spiral of reinforced avoidance. Although avoiding public speaking may not be too disruptive for many people, imagine if you had to speak in public as a part of your job—for example, if you were a teacher.

Situational Analysis Worksheet 3

Name: *Andy*

Date of Situational Event: *March 4, 2004*

Situational Area: ______ Family ______ Work/School __✓__ Social

---

Instructions: Select a stressful situation that has occurred in your life during the previous week. Please describe the situation using the steps indicated below.

---

1. Describe what happened:
   Beth told me that she was going to a club with her friends to dance and drink. She did not invite me to join them, but suggested that I hook up with some of my friends for a "boys' night out." I told her to have a good time.

2. Describe your interpretation(s) of what happened:
   ~~*1. Beth should know that I would want her to invite me along.*~~
   ~~*2. I'm not going to tell her that I'm upset because she'll just get angry.*~~
   ~~*3. She'd rather hang out with her friends than me, like she doesn't even like me any more.*~~
   - It's not that she doesn't have fun with me, she just wants some time alone with her friends.
   - It's possible she doesn't know much this hurts my feelings.
   - I need to tell her how I feel about this.

3. Describe what you did during the situation:
   ~~*1. All I said was for her to have fun. I didn't ask if I could come along.*~~
   ~~*2. Tone of voice: "defeated". I didn't sound happy when she left.*~~
   ~~*3. I wouldn't look at her or smile. I just ignored her and watched TV.*~~
   - Tell her something is bothering me and that I'd like to talk about it.
   - Use an assertive tone of voice.
   - Look directly at her when speaking.

4. Describe how you wanted the event to come out for you (Desired Outcome):
   I wanted to stand up for myself by telling her I felt rejected and lonely when she left me out of her plans tonight.

5. Describe how the event came out for you (Actual Outcome):
   I stayed at home alone while Beth went out. I felt miserable.

RATE: Did you get what you wanted? Yes ____ No __*X*__

FIG. 8.3. Situational Analysis Worksheet 3. Figure adapted from McCullough (2000) by Andrea B. Burns, Lorraine R. Reitzel, and Thomas E. Joiner Jr.

Having this type of anxiety would be extremely distressing. SA is helpful for people with anxiety because it helps elucidate the connection between (often catastrophic) thoughts and subsequent behaviors, such as avoidance. Practicing alternative thoughts and behaviors in the remedial phase of SA helps anxious individuals replace thoughts that do not work (hurtful thoughts) with more functional (helpful) thoughts, in turn increasing the chances of obtaining their DO. For further reading on how SA can be helpful with anxiety problems, please see section C of the Appendix.

Another complaint many people have is difficulty managing their anger. They describe blowing up at others with little provocation; saying or doing things they later regret; and getting into trouble at home, at work, or with the police. When SA is used to address anger management issues, an extra step is added to the technique, one that considers how your interpretations of a situation make you feel. So, SA with anger management includes consideration of a person's feelings and emotions. SA is a good technique to help people with problems managing their anger because it helps them to cue into how their thoughts are directly linked to how they feel, and how both thoughts and feelings influence their behavior in ways that are counterproductive to obtaining their DO. For more information on how SA works with anger management issues, and a case example with completed worksheets, see the first part of section D of the Appendix.

If you feel like you would like to get more of a sense how SA works with different types of problems, and how SA can help you with your problems, you may find the Appendix helpful. In addition to the issues described earlier, the Appendix describes SA with people who repeatedly experience interpersonal problems with others (section A), SA for parents and children experiencing problems getting along (section B), and SA for people in correctional environments (second part of section D). However, if you don't find the issue that you are struggling with described explicitly in the Appendix, remember that SA can be helpful for a wide variety of problems in a wide variety of settings, only a few examples of which are outlined in this workbook. The key is to apply the technique properly to your unique situation. In following Andy and Beth's example throughout this workbook, you already know everything you need to know to begin to apply SA to your life and its unique circumstances. All you need is a specific (stressful) situation and a DO to get yourself started and, with a little patience and lots of practice, soon you will see the power you possess to make situations in your life begin to turn out the way you want them to.

APPENDICES: ILLUSTRATIVE APPLICATIONS OF SITUATIONAL ANALYSIS

Appendix A

Personality Disorders

Many people find themselves having difficulty in interactions with friends, family, and coworkers. This may include a variety of problems that lead to social isolation, stormy and intense relationships, chronic feelings of anger and irritation at other people, and difficulty managing emotions. A variety of disorders result in problems such as these. If you have had symptoms such as these beginning in late adolescence and continuing into adulthood, you may fit the diagnostic criteria for a personality disorder. Personality disorders tend to include a chronic or constant pattern of difficulties. For a comprehensive diagnostic interview to determine whether you meet the criteria for a personality disorder, consult a mental health professional.

To manage the problems you may experience when interacting with other people, you may find Situational Analysis (SA) helpful (see Fig. A.1). SA teaches you how to get what you want in specific situations. Many people find that they have a ready supply of thoughts that result in negative emotions when interacting with other people. SA will arm you with the skills you need to begin thinking in ways that will counteract those hurtful thoughts. You may also find that you often act and react in ways that get you into trouble. This method will teach you to act in ways that help you get you what you want rather than what you don't want. Although SA will teach you how to do this one situation at a time, you will begin to notice changes in many areas of your life as you begin to apply these techniques more globally.

Situational Analysis Worksheet

Name: ______________________________

Date of Situational Event: ______________________________

Situational Area: _______ Family _______ Work/School _______ Social

Instructions: Select one stressful event that has happened to you during the past week and describe it using the format below. Please try to fill out **all** parts of the questionnaire.

1. Describe what happened:

2. Describe your interpretation(s) of what happened:

3. Describe what you did during the situation:

4. Describe how you wanted the event to come out for you (Desired Outcome):

5. Describe how the event came out for you (Actual Outcome):

RATE: Was the desired outcome achieved? Yes ____ No ____

FIG. A.1. Situational Analysis Worksheet. Figure adapted from McCullough (2000) by Kelly C. Cukrowicz.

This part of the appendix is divided into sections that focus on Borderline Personality Disorder, Passive–Aggressive Personality Disorder, and Schizotypal Personality Disorder. Each section includes diagnostic criteria, information on how to apply SA to your own life situations, and illustrative case material.

BORDERLINE PERSONALITY DISORDER

Borderline Personality Disorder (BPD) is defined by the *Diagnostic and Statistical Manual of Mental Disorders* as "a pervasive pattern of instability of interpersonal relationships, self-image, and affects, and a marked impulsivity beginning by early adulthood and present in a variety of contexts" (American Psychiatric Association, 1994, p. 654). For example, a person with BPD may have stormy relationships with others as a result of anticipating that the person will abandon him or her. Difficulty with impulsivity and emotional control might lead an individual to self-harming behavior or persistent thoughts of suicide. In addition, it is common for people with BPD to alternate between extremes, such as love and hate. SA may be an effective treatment for symptoms of BPD. As you learned in the main chapters of this workbook, completing SA worksheets may help you to get more of what you want out of life. Specifically, problems associated with BPD may be tackled as specific situations in SA. These problems may arise through reactions to thoughts associated with BPD. Such thinking patterns are described in more detail in Fig. A.2.

Behaviors that may result from BPD-style thoughts include actions that lead to stormy relationships with important people in your life. For example, alternating between behaviors that show affection (i.e., love) and distaste (i.e., hate) may leave loved ones feeling frustrated and irritated. Self-harming behavior also causes stress in relationships. As loved ones acclimate themselves to the fear that the person with BPD might harm him- or herself, they stop responding with alarm to these instances of self-harm. The person with BPD is then left feeling unloved and abandoned. How do you change this? You begin to complete SA worksheets when things are going lousy for you. These worksheets will help you to break the situation down, examine your thoughts, review your behaviors, and figure out what got in your way.

As an example of a way of thinking that prevents you from getting what you want, you may tend to evaluate desired outcomes (DOs) and actual outcomes (AOs) in ways that reflect black-and-white thinking. In other

Theme Area	Example of Specific Thought
Abandonment	"I'll be alone forever. No one will be there for me."
Unlovability	"No one would love me or want to be close to me if they really got to know me."
Dependence	"I can't cope on my own. I need someone to rely on."
Subjugation/Lack of Individuation	"I must oppress my wants to the desires of others or they'll abandon me or attack me."
Mistrust	"People will hurt me, attack me, take advantage of me. I must protect myself."
Inadequate Self-Discipline	"It isn't possible for me to control myself or discipline myself."
Fear of Losing Emotional Control	"I must control my emotions or something terrible will happen to me."
Guilt/Punishment	"I'm a bad person. I deserve to be punished."
Emotional Deprivation	"No one is ever there to meet my needs, to be strong for me, to care for me."

FIG. A.2. Common thoughts associated with Borderline Personality Disorder.

words, you might tend to identify entirely positive DOs for interpersonal interactions and tend to report AOs that you see as entirely negative. This means that you rarely pay attention to positive things that you accomplish; instead, you often think only about positive things you *wish* you had accomplished. One goal of SA is to begin to evaluate these outcomes more objectively. How do you do this? First, you can use your behavior in your descriptions. For example, rather than stating "I wanted to feel happy" as a DO, you substitute "I wanted to do . . ." This will help you avoid the patterns of black-and-white thinking previously described. By reflecting on the gulf between your DO and your AO, you may be able to learn how to challenge your black-and-white thinking about specific situations.

You may also have problems with feelings of loss, mistrust, and guilt. You should be on the lookout for these themes in Step 2 of your SA worksheets. Using SA, you can challenge these interpretations by questioning whether they seemed to help or hinder your progress toward your DOs. Although it is sometimes difficult to experience these emotions, an honest evaluation of them may be helpful in revising interpretations that are not helpful. As you have learned thus far, the primary application of SA is that it helps you get more of what you want in specific situations.

The second application of SA occurs when you use it to respond to crises. This application focuses almost exclusively on the interpretations that you made during the crisis and the specific behaviors in which you engaged. In this manner, SA can help teach you what happens when you respond in certain ways and how this influences your emotions. You will learn the connections between the things that cause a crisis for you. Learning SA will help you to control your thoughts and actions so that you can stop yourself from feeling out of control in these situations. When you are starting to learn the SA approach, you may struggle to use this in crisis situations, but as you become more familiar with this technique you will be able to apply it with greater success.

The final application of SA is when you use it to understand conflicts that occur during interpersonal encounters. Here, the goal is to use SA to highlight disruptive interpretations, behaviors, and DOs during a real-time interpersonal encounter. This is likely to be the most challenging application for you, as you must deal with the strong emotions elicited by interpersonal conflict, and therefore it is recommended for the later stages of treatment.

In these three ways, using the SA approach may be helpful to you. Specifically, the key ingredients of SA target BPD's essential features. The steps of SA teach you a mindful, planful approach to interpersonal situations. Monitoring your thoughts and behaviors may help you regulate your mood so that you feel less vulnerable to ups and downs. By mastering such an approach, you can improve your impulse control. Finally, focusing on DOs may help you resolve identity problems.

Case Example

Brian is a 26-year-old, single, Caucasian man. He did not graduate from high school; however, he subsequently earned a general equivalency diploma. He has worked a variety of jobs throughout his adult life and is currently employed through a temporary agency as an office assistant. Brian complains of a variety of symptoms, including mood swings, low self-esteem, difficulties in both family and dating relationships, anxiety and worry, guilt, substance abuse, sleep difficulties, and chronic feelings of sadness and lack of motivation. He reported thoughts of suicide dating back to age 16 with at least five suicide attempts, including cutting his wrists, swallowing pills, and jumping off a two-story building. Brian met with a therapist to determine whether he was experiencing the symptoms of a personality disorder. His therapist indicated that he met the criteria for BPD. Brian decided to continue therapy beyond the initial diagnostic interview to learn how to apply SA to manage his symptoms. The following SA (see Fig. A.3) and transcript are from a therapy session with Brian.

Brian's Situational Analysis Worksheet

Name: ______________________________

Date of Situational Event: ______________________________

Situational Area: _______ Family _______ Work/School ___✓___ Social

---

Instructions: Select one stressful event that has happened to you during the past week and describe it using the format below. Please try to fill out **all** parts of the questionnaire.

---

1. Describe what happened:

   My girlfriend and I had an argument about her going back to Mexico for that missionary work that she does. When we were done arguing, I tried to hold her hand, but she said wouldn't let me because she said it's against her religion.

2. Describe your interpretation(s) of what happened:

   - Why can't I show affection?
   - I know she's kissing other men in Mexico.
   - We've kissed in the past, but everything has changed since she returned from Mexico the first time.

3. Describe what you did during the situation:

   - I told her to kiss her Mexican friends.
   - I turned away from her.
   - I said, "if you leave now, then it's over for good!"
   - I also told her that if she left I would kill myself.

4. Describe how you wanted the event to come out for you (Desired Outcome):

   That she would have stayed to discuss it.

5. Describe how the event came out for you (Actual Outcome):

   She left and I got drunk and went to the store and bought a bottle of sleeping pills.

RATE: Was the desired outcome achieved? Yes _____ No __*X*__

FIG. A.3. Brian's Situational Analysis Worksheet. Figure adapted from McCullough (2000) by Kelly C. Cukrowicz, Sarah A. Shultz, and Keith F. Donohue.

Therapist (T): OK, Brian, I see that you've brought in your homework assignment for today. Why don't you go ahead and tell me about the situation that you outlined on the SA worksheet. I'm going to write it down here as you're describing it, so that I can make sure that I get all of the details.

Brian (B): My girlfriend Andi and I had an argument about her going back to Mexico for that missionary work that she does. When we were done arguing, I tried to hold her hand, but she said she wouldn't let me because she said it's against her religion.

T: OK, let me make sure I have this right. . . . First, you and Andi had an argument. Following the argument, you tried to hold her hand, but she would not allow you to do that based on her religious beliefs. Do I have that right?

B: Yes, that's basically what happened.

T: Okay, now tell me your thoughts and interpretations of that situation. One way to do this is to fill in the blank, "When I was there in that situation, it meant ______." Tell me what this situation meant to you.

B: Well, I thought to myself, "Why can't I show affection?"

T: So, to you, holding hands would be a sign of affection.

B: Yeah, holding hands is a sign of affection, and what's wrong with that?

T: OK, good, that's a good one. Did you have any other interpretations?

B: Yeah . . . I know she's kissing other men in Mexico.

T: OK; you thought to yourself, "I know she's kissing other men in Mexico." What is your interpretation of that thought? What does that mean to you?

B: She's cheating on me.

T: OK, so when you were in the situation and Andi refused to hold your hand, you thought to yourself, "I know she's cheating on me in Mexico and kissing other men." Did you have any other thoughts or interpretations?

B: We've kissed in the past, but everything has changed since she returned from Mexico the first time.

T: OK, so that's good, now we have three interpretations to work with. Let's go on to Step 3. What were your behaviors? When you tried to hold Andi's hand and she would not let you, what did you say and do in the situation?

B: I told her to go and kiss her Mexican friends!

T: And how did you say that, what was your tone?

B: I don't know, I just said it.

T: If I was a fly on the wall, what would I have seen and heard?

B: I guess I sounded sort of sarcastic or cocky, like, fine . . . whatever . . . go kiss whoever you want, I don't care!

T: OK, I think I can picture it. What else did you say and do?

B: I turned away from her.

T: Did you say anything else?

B: Well, when she got up to leave I said, "If you leave now, then it's over for good!" I also told her that if she left I would kill myself.

T: And what was your tone when you said that?

B: The same as before; I wasn't really yelling, but I was letting her know that I was angry.

T: OK, so your tone was angry and forceful.

B: Yeah, I wanted her to know that I was serious.

T: So, let me make sure I have all of this down. After you and Andi had an argument, you reached out to her and tried to hold her hand, but she would not hold your hand because she felt is was against her religious beliefs. You responded by turning away from her and telling her to go kiss her Mexican friends. When she got up to leave, you told her that if she left, it would be over between you for good and that you would kill yourself.

B: Well, when you say it like that it sounds bad.

T: I'm not trying to make it sound bad or good; I just want to make sure that I have an accurate account of the facts.

B: Yeah, I guess that's what happened . . . but it wasn't my fault.

T: No one is assigning blame here, Brian. What did you want to happen; what was your DO?

B: That she would have stayed to discuss it.

T: So what you wanted was for Andi to stay and discuss what had just happened. Is that about right?

B: Yes.

T: Let's go on and see how this situation ended up. What was the AO in this situation?

B: She left and I got drunk and went to the store and bought a bottle of sleeping pills.

T: Did you take the pills?

B: No.

T: What kept you from taking the pills?

B: I passed out before I had a chance to take them.

T: So, it sounds like there were some other thoughts going on in Step 2 that we missed the first time through.

B: What do you mean?

T: How did you get from her getting up to leave to telling her you were going to kill yourself? What were you thinking?

B: "If I tell her I'm going to kill myself, she'll stay."

T: Let me write that down . . . OK, we'll come back to that in a few minutes. So you know what comes next . . . did you get what you wanted in this situation?

B: NO!!!

T: Okay, now let's look at each thought and interpretation to see whether it helped you or hurt you in getting your DO of Andi staying to discuss the situation with you. The first thing you told me was that you thought, "Why can't I show affection?" Did that thought help you or hurt you in achieving your DO of Andi staying to discuss the situation?

B: I don't know; I don't really think it hurt.

T: I'm not sure either. Let's put it this way . . . do you think it helped you to get Andi to stay?

B: I guess not.

T: I don't think so, either; what do you think you could have thought instead?

B: I don't know . . . maybe, "I really want to show her how much I care about her."

T: Good! I think that's a great thought! Can you think of any more?

B: Holding hands is a sign of affection . . . I just still don't understand why we are not allowed to touch each other!

T: What could you have thought that could have helped you understand her beliefs?

B: Maybe . . . I don't know, maybe I should ask her to explain her religion to me.

T: Great!!! It seems to me that thinking "I really want to show her how much I care about her" and "I should ask her to explain her religion to me" would have helped you to get your DO of Andi staying to discuss things with you.

T: Now, since we're running low on time, let's look at your thoughts, "I know she's cheating on me and kissing other men in Mexico" and "We've kissed in the past, but everything has changed since she returned from Mexico" together. Do you think those thoughts helped you or hurt you in achieving your DO of Andi staying to discuss the situation with you?

B: I think those probably hurt, because they just pissed me off.

T: I agree with that. What would have been a more helpful interpretation?

B: (*pause*) Maybe that's the way people great each other in Mexico.

T: OK, that's great! What are some other helpful thoughts?

B: I trust Andi, she loves me.

T: Beautiful! It sounds to me that if you were thinking those thoughts, it definitely would have helped you to achieve your DO. Now let's look at the thought, "If I tell her I'm going to kill myself, she'll stay." Do you think that one helped you or hurt you?

B: I guess it hurt.

T: You don't sound convinced.

B: It's just hard to give that one up.

T: I know, Brian, that's been an effective strategy for you for a long time now. But, I agree with you, it didn't help you to achieve your DO in this situation. What do you think you could have thought instead?

B: I don't know . . . I don't think there was anything I could have thought that would really have made her stay.

T: I know this is hard, but just try to think about some helpful thoughts that may have helped you to regulate your emotions and the way you were interacting with her.

B: Maybe just thinking, "I really want her to stay and talk to me."

T: That sounds good. Is there anything else?

B: How about, "I want us to work this out!"?

T: I think that's a great one! You are really getting better at this! I know it is hard to generate these kinds of thoughts, especially in the heat of the moment, but you are doing a great job so far, and it's only going to get easier the more we practice! Let's move on to your behaviors . . . you said that you told her, "Why don't you go kiss your Mexican friends!" I think that we can agree that that wasn't a helpful thing to say. What could you have said to help you get your DO of Andi staying to talk with you?

B: Maybe I could have asked her to explain why she doesn't want to hold my hand . . . to explain the rules of her religion to me.

T: I think that would have been a helpful thing to say. I know we're sort of rushing through this, but I think you are getting the hang of it. Let's move on to the last thing you said, "If you leave now, then it's over for good and I'm going to kill myself!" Do you think that one was helpful or hurtful?

B: We both know it was hurtful.

T: What could you have said instead?

B: "Andi, I just really want you to stay and talk to me!"

T: Good, is there anything else?

B: I could have told her that I love her, I guess.

T: I agree, Brian, I think that would have helped you get your DO. Now let's wrap things up . . . what have you learned from this situation?

B: I guess that, if I want to work things out with Andi, I need to be honest about how I feel and to be respectful to her. Threatening to kill myself is not fair to her and, at least in this situation, didn't get me what I wanted.

T: Good work today. I know this isn't easy for you, but you're making a lot of progress. Keep working on these homework assignments, and it's only going to get easier! I'll see you next week.

Brian's case illustrates the possible utility of SA for problems associated with symptoms of BPD. Although this example was from the early stages of treatment, using SA helped Brian regulate his emotions; develop effective problem-solving techniques; stabilize his interpersonal relationships; and understand the link among his interpretations, behaviors, and the way people respond to him.

Summary and Conclusions

This section has presented information that you can use in conjunction with the main chapters of this workbook for symptoms of BPD. Specifically, as you identify themes of thinking that cause you difficulty in relationships, you can begin to generate alternative thoughts that will help you to get more of what you want in specific situations. You can also generate alternative behaviors that are more consistent with your DOs. As you become more successful in applying this technique, you will feel more in control of your relationships, your emotions, and your thoughts about yourself and others.

PASSIVE–AGGRESSIVE PERSONALITY DISORDER

Passive–Aggressive Personality Disorder (PAPD) is characterized by a pervasive pattern of passive resistance and negative reactivity. This may include, for example, passive refusal to complete tasks required by superiors or behaving in a verbally aggressive way while neglecting to be forthright about a concern with a loved one. Passive–aggressive tendencies may be detrimental and interfere with interpersonal, social, and occupational functioning. If you have these symptoms, others may reject you in personal relationships or terminate you from work positions because of your oppositional behavior. If rejections and terminations become frequent, your life functioning may deteriorate significantly. For this reason, passive–aggressive tendencies should not be ignored or go untreated.

If you have passive–aggressive tendencies, you may have recurrent thoughts that revolve around themes such as rebelling against authority and predicting negative outcomes (see Fig. A.4 for examples). These thoughts may reveal anger and rigidity that you often feel when interacting with other people. To undertake changing these recurrent thoughts, you may begin by evaluating both the evidence that supports your thoughts and evidence that refutes them. For example, if you believe that your teacher was wrong to assign a task for homework, you may think of alternate beliefs that support your belief as well as alternatives that do not. This will allow you to make a more objective decision about how you will behave and whether you will complete the assignment. In addition, you

- Authority figures tend to be intrusive, demanding, interfering, or controlling.
- Being controlled or dominated by others is intolerable.
- Rules are arbitrary and stifle me.
- Other people are often too demanding.
- I am self-sufficient, but I do need others to help me reach my goals.

FIG. A.4. Thoughts typical of Passive–Aggressive Personality Disorder.

should start to evaluate the costs and benefits of holding those beliefs. A cost of not completing the assignment would be a lower grade. As you progress through SA, you should do the same for a potentially more adaptive belief. In the previous example, a benefit would be a higher grade and the respect of your teacher. In addition to the problematic beliefs that you hold, you may engage in patterns of behavior that are getting in the way of what you want (e.g., not completing the assignment would get in the way of the goal of getting a high grade). These behaviors usually result in situational outcomes that contradict your goals.

The five-step SA approach is ideally suited to the treatment of PAPD, for a number of reasons. For example, the second step of the approach—"What did the situation mean to you?"—focuses you on your thoughts during specific situations. This technique helps you identify passive–aggressive interpretations (e.g., "I don't have to do what authorities tell me!") you made during these situations. Identification of these thoughts and interpretations is helpful, because you may not have been aware of them or of how frequently they occur. You also may not have observed how your passive–aggressive thoughts lead to both passive–aggressive behaviors and unfavorable situational outcomes. Step 2 of SA illustrates these connections explicitly. When you look back at your interpretations during several situations, you may be able to point out the frequent recurrence of certain passive–aggressive thoughts and make generalized conclusions about how such thoughts typically lead to passive–aggressive behaviors and negative situational outcomes.

Likewise, Step 3 of SA—"What did you do in the situation?"—helps you identify patterns of passive–aggressive behaviors and recognize how these lead you toward negative results. This technique is especially well suited to PAPD because passive–aggressive behaviors may not be readily apparent to you or even to others with whom you interact. Specifically, it is often what you are *not* doing that is of more significance than what you are doing. Although this point seems so simple, comprehending this pattern can be a very profound experience. It may seem very simple or obvious to think about whether your *inaction* helped you to get what you wanted (DO), yet it is precisely this question that creates a feeling of disharmony in you and motivates you to change your behavior to more active approaches.

The elicitation phase of SA helps you to understand that your passive–aggressive thoughts and behaviors are not working. In the remediation phase, on the other hand, you learn to generate alternative thoughts and behaviors that are more helpful in achieving your DOs than the passive–aggressive thoughts and behaviors that you used routinely before using SA. Through repeated experiences with the remediation phase of SA, and through using the alternative thoughts and behaviors you generate in real situations, you can ultimately change your characteristically passive–aggressive strategies.

In the remediation phase of SA, you should begin to replace negative thoughts about authorities and others at Step 2 with thoughts that focus you on completing tasks that you may not enjoy but which you nonetheless must complete to obtain some greater DO. In addition, remediation of behaviors at Step 3 should emphasize the use of assertive communication and efficient completion of tasks.

Case Example

Joe is a 24-year-old graduate student. He reported a period of four months of major depression in his first year in his program. He recalled staying in his house for much of this time and rarely attending classes. As a result, he was expelled. However, after some discussions with faculty, Joe was given a second chance in the program. Joe exhibited strong tendencies to (a) resent authorities and see them as arbitrary, (b) procrastinate on assigned tasks, (c) make many "false starts" without completion, and (d) express resentment and anger through passive–aggressive behaviors.

When completing SAs with Joe, the focus was on his tendency to avoid working on homework in certain classes. Figure A.5 presents a SA from one session with Joe, and the following is a partial transcript of the session:

Therapist (T): OK! So, we know that you have had this assignment a long time and that it's overdue. How about we look at one time when you were working on the assignment?

Joe (J): Well, a couple of nights ago I finally sat down at my desk and looked at the assignment. I spent a couple hours trying to get a free copy of the stupid

Joe's Situational Analysis Worksheet

Name: ______________________________

Date of Situational Event: ______________________________

Situational Area: ________ Family ___✓___ Work/School ________ Social

Instructions: Select one stressful event that has happened to you during the past week and describe it using the format below. Please try to fill out **all** parts of the questionnaire.

1. Describe what happened:
   - *I sat down to do my homework.*
   - *I thought about how unfair the assignment was.*
   - *I decided to do other things.*

2. Describe your interpretation(s) of what happened:
   - *This assignment is unfair because it requires a special program only available on campus that I can't download for use at home.*
   - *I shouldn't have to do this assignment.*
   - *There is no value to me for doing this assignment.*
   - *I'm being made to do something I don't want to do.*

3. Describe what you did during the situation:
   - *Sat down to do homework*
   - *Got up to do something else*

4. Describe how you wanted the event to come out for you (Desired Outcome):
   - *To complete my homework*

5. Describe how the event came out for you (Actual Outcome):
   - *Did not complete my homework*

RATE: Was the desired outcome achieved? Yes ____ No __*X*__

FIG. A.5. Joe's Situational Analysis Worksheet. Figure adapted from McCullough (2000) by Kelly C. Cukrowicz, Mark Reeves, and Marisol Perez.

computer program we have to use and I couldn't find it on the Internet. The whole assignment is a waste of time because it's nothing like what I'll actually be doing.

T: OK. I wrote that you sat down to do your homework and decided it was unfair. What else happened in the situation?

J: (*Silence. Stares intensely at the therapist.*) I didn't do it.

T: OK. You didn't do it. So, you did something else instead, right?

J: Yeah, I went and watched TV.

T: That's Step 1. We made a very brief, bulleted description of the situation. Now let's go to Step 2. What did the situation mean to you? What were you thinking?

J: I was thinking how stupid the assignment was. I couldn't understand why I had to go and use this program when there are other, more common programs that I would actually use in real life. I was thinking this assignment was useless to me since it's artificial and doesn't relate to my work. Overall, I was thinking that I was being forced to do something that I really didn't want to do.

T: OK. Got that down. That's Step 2, your thoughts. Now let's go to Step 3, your behaviors. What did you do in the situation? It sounds like you sat down to do your homework, didn't do your homework, then got up to do something else. What did you want in the situation?

J: To finish the assignment.

T: What was the end result of the situation, the outcome?

J: I didn't do my homework.

T: OK, so like we said before: You don't like this assignment, but you know it will help you pass this class so you won't get kicked out of your program again. Did you get what you wanted?

J: (*Long silence. Stares intensely at ground, then at therapist.*) No.

T: Now, let's look back at your thoughts and behaviors to see if they were helpful or hurtful. Did thinking to yourself, "This assignment is unfair because it requires a special program only available on campus that I can't download for use at home" help you or hurt you to get the assignment done?

J: I guess it didn't help.

T: Makes sense. If you feel the assignment is unfair, you'd probably feel kinda pissed and not want to do the thing. How about the other thoughts, "I shouldn't have to do the assignment," "There is no value to me for doing this assignment," "I'm being made to do something I don't want to do"? Did those help or hurt?

J: They didn't help. They just made me more pissed off at this stupid assignment.

T: OK. How about your behaviors? Did sitting down at the table help?

J: No.

T: Well, OK. But at least you're sitting down to work on it, right? Instead of totally avoiding your desk?

J: I guess.

T: So, that's a tough one, but I'd say it actually helped. How about getting up to do something else?

J: Obviously that didn't help.

T: Right. Let's go back over this situation to see if you could have thought or done anything differently to get what you wanted. So, what else could you have thought to get what you wanted? Again, I'm not trying to tell you what you should want, and I'm not arguing that you have to do what other people want. I'm assuming that you wanted to get the assignment done. What else could you have thought?

J: (*Silence.*) I don't know. I didn't want to do it.

T: OK, how about "I really don't want to do this crappy assignment, but I have to if I want to pass this stupid class. I guess I'd better just do the stupid thing so I can move on."

J: (*Laughs.*) Yeah, I guess that would help. But it's hard to think those things. I know I should think them, but I don't. I keep thinking how stupid the assignment is.

T: That's totally normal, and it's why you're here. Listen, if you practice this thing we're doing, you will eventually come to think and do things that will at least help you get what you want in every situation, at every moment in your life. The thoughts here on the paper are knee-jerk for you. You automatically think them every time you get what you see as a dumb assignment. If you keep practicing the helpful thoughts, though, they will hopefully become automatic and replace the hurtful thoughts. OK, now let's look at your behavior.

J: Well that's obvious. Not doing the homework didn't help me do the homework.

T: Yeah, this stuff is kind of common sense, but it helps to really look at what you're doing in each situation to see if it's helping you or hurting you. Well, OK. So, what else could you have done?

J: Just do the damn assignment.

T: Yeah . . . I think that would help. (*Smiles.*)

J: You know, I have all these different thoughts. I think about trying to change the system. I think about what else I could be doing. I think about what I'd do if I were in charge. I wonder if things from my past are making me not do this stuff. I'm not sure what the right thing is to think!

T: Yeah, we could come up with all kinds of ways of looking at this, right? We could come up with lots of different theories and speculate about why you do these things. You know what, though? It really comes down to one simple question: Does it help, or does it hurt? Is thinking this helping me to get what I want, or hurting me?

These thoughts seemed to lead Joe toward behaviors in which he refused to comply with demands that he perceived as unfair and coming from arbitrary authorities. The end result, however, was to take Joe one step closer to again being expelled from his program. He stated that he wanted to complete the program, which now required obtaining a high grade in all of his classes to make up for his poor grades. Examining the thoughts and behaviors Joe chose in this situation revealed that none of them helped him to complete his homework, and all of them hurt him in achieving this DO. However, Joe was able to understand that choosing other thoughts and behaviors could help him achieve his DO.

Summary and Conclusions

By now you have probably discovered that SA is ideally suited to treating PAPD. The treatment effectively uncovers your passive–aggressive thoughts and behaviors that may not have been readily apparent you or to others. SA also uniquely highlights how such thoughts and behaviors are counterproductive through repeated evaluations of your effectiveness in achieving situational DOs. The end result is that you can become an active participant in your life and obtain directly and assertively what you truly desire.

SCHIZOTYPAL PERSONALITY DISORDER

Schizotypal Personality Disorder (STPD) is a pattern of maladaptive interpersonal behavior characterized by certain cognitive and behavioral symptoms. This may include few, if any, social relationships as a result of discomfort in social situations and minimal social skills. Individuals with STPD have difficulty establishing close relationships because of their odd behavior and thoughts, which may include strange or "magical" beliefs about life and how things occur. For example, a person with STPD may be superstitious or preoccupied with paranormal phenomena that are outside the norms of his or her subculture. He or she may also believe that he or she has magical control over others. These symptoms result in extreme discomfort and a diminished capacity to form close relationships. SA appears to be a particularly promising approach in the treatment of STPD symptoms, for several reasons. First, if you have schizotypal personality symptoms, you may repeatedly encounter situations that result in undesirable outcomes, and SA is designed to help you identify the thoughts and behaviors that are contributing to those unwanted outcomes. Second, SA involves regular completion of the SA worksheet, which increases your control over life's events so you can better manage your interpersonal environment. Separate examination of behaviors, thoughts, and their connection to specific outcomes can make complex and abstract life events simpler and more concrete.

We recommend several modifications to the general SA approach to address the characteristic symptoms of STPD (see Fig. A.6). First, you should select a very specific and brief slice of time for each SA worksheet. To evaluate adherence to this direction, record the duration of selected situations (in minutes). You may find that sticking to one or two sentences is also helpful in your description. Second, you should try to select only the most important interpretations and behaviors in Steps 2 and 3. Third, you should pay particular attention to separating the DO from your description of the situation. Separating these may help you feel less confused about the separate parts of the SA worksheet. You may find that you have a difficult time completing the SA worksheet with brief descriptions. If so, rate each thought or behavior on a scale of 1 (*least applicable*) to 10 (*most applicable*). Then keep the most applicable thoughts and behaviors on your SA worksheet. Fourth, take care to note any behaviors that you think others might find odd or eccentric. These symptoms of STPD often contribute significantly to your ineffective navigation of social situations. Finally, you should attempt to seek feedback from others in terms of their impressions of your communications after completion of SA worksheets.

Case Example

Karl is a 20-year-old, never-married, Caucasian college student. He has a long history of difficulty with others dating back to his childhood. When Karl commenced therapy, he told his therapist that he felt that others always described him as weird. He acknowledged that he sometimes says odd things and has difficulty feeling at ease with other people. This appeared to hold especially true for individuals whom he perceived as attractive, educated, and poised. Karl commonly categorized people in this fashion, perhaps promoting a sense of separation and differentness from others. His social network was largely restricted to family members. His approach to meeting women was rather haphazard and almost accidental, but he idealized these encounters as "magical."

Karl also exhibited noticeably odd behaviors that compromised his communications with others. For example, he tended to vocalize every thought that occurred to him in explaining a situation, as if each were

Situational Analysis Worksheet for Schizotypal Personality

Name: ____

Date of Situational Event: ______________________________________

Situational Area: ______ Family ______ Work/School ______ Social

Instructions: Select one stressful event that has happened to you during the past week and describe it using the format below. Please try to fill out **all** parts of the questionnaire.

1. In two or three sentences, describe the situation.

2. What was your interpretation of the situation? What did this situation mean to you?
   a.
   b.
   c.
   d.

3. What were your behaviors in this situation?
   a. Eye Contact -
   b. Body Posture -
   c. Gestures -
   d. Tone of Voice -
   e. Timing -
   f. Other behaviors -

   What did you say? How did you say it?

4. State what you wanted to get out of this situation. What was your desired outcome?

5. What was the actual outcome of this situation?

RATE: Did you get what you wanted? Yes _____ No ______

FIG. A.6. Situational Analysis Worksheet for Schizotypal Personality. Figure adapted from McCullough (2000) by Maureen Lyons Reardon.

equally important to the communication. He showed particular difficulty staying focused and generally responded to questions in a rambling manner.

The following transcript presents a situation in which Karl reported having difficulty interacting with a fellow classmate (see Fig. A.7):

Therapist (T): All right, Karl, let's look at your worksheet. Why don't we start with Step 1?

Karl (K): OK. Well, I wrote down that I was sitting in class when I noticed Jenn nearby. I tried to talk to her, but she didn't say much. I gave up.

T: Great. Last week when you described the situation you had a really hard time being concise. That was much better. I asked you to use the fly on the wall criterion, and you did a good job with that.

K: Well, I was just thinking about Jenn, and she is so nice that I just wanted to be able to talk to her more. I thought maybe she'd like to go out with me—you know, these things are always fate anyway. She probably already doesn't like me. She might just think I'm a strange person.

T: Hang on a second for me. One of the things we agreed to work on is staying on task in our sessions. We were talking about Step 1. Let's get back to that.

K: Right, I know. OK. Shoot.

T: You ended with "I gave up." Tell me what that looked like.

K: Well, I turned back around in my seat after it got a little quiet between us.

T: Let's move on to Step 2. What were your interpretations? In other words, what did the situation mean to you?

K: I wrote a few things down. "She thinks I'm weird." "I don't have anything in common with her." And then, "Fate will control how this comes out."

T: Great. Those are good interpretations for us to work with. Let's keep going. What did you write for Step 3? What were your behaviors in the situation?

K: Ummm. I said a few things to her. I started by turning toward her and clearing my throat. Then I asked her what she was up to. I tried to talk to her about the class. Then I turned back around when she didn't seem interested.

T: OK, that's great. Let me ask you a few questions. What was her response when you asked her what she was up to?

K: She rolled her eyes and said she was waiting for class to start.

T: Then what did you say?

K: I asked her what she thought of the class. Whether she liked reading the textbook. Things like that.

T: OK. And she didn't seem interested, right?

K: Yeah, I don't know why she wasn't. Maybe it just wasn't meant to be. You know, like it isn't fate for us to connect.

T: Let's get back to your worksheet. What did you want to get out of this situation? What was your DO?

Karl's Situational Analysis Worksheet for Schizotypal Personality

Name: ____________________

Date of Situational Event: *June 15, 2004*

Situational Area: _______ Family _______ Work/School ___✓___ Social

Instructions: Select one stressful event that has happened to you during the past week and describe it using the format below. Please try to fill out **all** parts of the questionnaire.

1. In two or three sentences, describe the situation.

   I was sitting in class when I noticed Jenn nearby. I tried to talk to her but she didn't say much. I gave up.

2. What was your interpretation of the situation? What did this situation mean to you?

   a. *She thinks I'm weird.*
   b. *I don't have anything in common with her.*
   c. *Fate will control how this comes out.*

3. What were your behaviors in this situation?

   a. Eye Contact - *Not great. I was nervous.*
   b. Body Posture - *A little slumped.*
   c. Gestures - *None.*
   d. Tone of Voice - *Kind of quiet.*
   e. Timing -
   f. Other behaviors -

   What did you say? How did you say it?

   I asked her what she was up to.

4. State what you wanted to get out of this situation. What was your desired outcome?

   For it to be fated.

5. What was the actual outcome of this situation?

   It wasn't fate.

RATE: Did you get what you wanted? Yes ____ No __*X*__

FIG. A.n7. Karl's Situational Analysis Worksheet for Schizotypal Personality. Figure adapted from McCullough (2000) by Maureen Lyons Reardon and Kelly C. Cukrowicz.

K: I wanted her to be fated for me.

T: Let's talk a little about DOs. I would like you to see if you can describe that DO in a different way. Imagine for me that you got what you wanted out of the situation. If I were watching what would I have seen?

K: She would have been interested in what I had to say. We would have had a good conversation.

T: Tell me what actually happened?

K: I wrote down that it wasn't fate.

T: Again, what would I have seen actually happen?

K: She wasn't interested in me, so I gave up on talking to her.

T: OK; did you get what you wanted?

K: No. Not at all.

T: OK. Let's talk about why you didn't get what you wanted then. I know you said it wasn't fate. For now, can we look at your interpretations and behaviors and see if those might have had anything to do with the AO? Can you do that?

K: Sure. I know you don't always agree with my reasons. OK, so where do we start?

T: Let's begin with your interpretations. Your first interpretation was that she thinks you are weird. Did that help you or hurt you in getting your DO?

K: I think it must have been bad. Since I thought she was thinking I was weird, I probably had a hard time being comfortable. That might have made her less interested, because I asked her an obvious question that bored her.

T: OK, your second interpretation, "I don't have anything in common with her." Did that help you to get what you wanted?

K: I think that one wasn't good either. I was so awkward because I felt I didn't anything in common with her.

T: And the last one was that fate will control how it comes out.

K: I guess fate isn't that important to the actual situation. It's just important to me.

T: These interpretations were all hurtful to your DO. Let's see if we can generate some helpful interpretations. What do you think?

K: How do I do that? That wasn't what I was thinking about it.

T: Maybe not. But let's see if we can generate some other things that might have been more helpful.

K: Well, I could have just thought she might like to talk to me. Or that maybe fate doesn't work on the first conversation with someone. Or that I might have lots in common with her.

T: Wow, great! That's a lot. What do you think about those? Would you have gotten your DO if you thought she might like to talk to you?

K: I don't know. Just thinking that wouldn't have made her interested.

T: OK—the next one, then. About fate. Was that helpful to your DO?

K: I know what you're getting at. This happened a few weeks ago. None of my helpful interpretations will help, right? Because I forgot to give you a DO that relies on my own behavior.

T: That's true, but let's be sure you followed my logic. Why does it matter?

K: You said because I can't control her reaction. I could try everything and she still might not be interested.

T: Great! OK. Next, to Step 3. Your behaviors. Tell me, which ones were helpful and which ones were hurtful to your DO?

K: I think I started out well. I got her attention so that I could ask her a question. But then I think it was silly to ask her about class. It wasn't interesting. I think that hurt me. I gave up easily, too. Maybe I could have just changed the subject and asked her something else.

T: OK, so if you had asked her something more interesting and persisted, would that would have resulted in your DO?

K: Maybe. I don't know. But I guess it doesn't matter what I did, huh? Her reaction was her reaction.

T: So, to end this, what would have been a DO that related to your behavior?

K: I guess I would just change that I would try to do my best to be interesting.

T: What would that look like?

K: I would have asked if she had done anything really fun lately.

T: Great. I know this was hard, but you did a great job. Really good work!

Karl's case illustrates the application of SA to a specific situation of relevance to someone with STPD. This situation makes clear how changing the way you think about the meaning of the situation and behave during the situation can help you get what you want. An important thing to remember is that you are always in control. You can always get what you want if you remember to aim for things that are under your control—that is, your thoughts and your behavior.

Summary and Conclusions

SA appears to be a particularly promising approach in the treatment of STPD symptoms, for several reasons. You may repeatedly encounter situations that result in undesirable outcomes, and SA is designed to assist you in identifying the thoughts and behaviors that are contributing to the unwanted outcomes in those situations. SA involves regular completion of the SA worksheet, which increases your control over life's events in order to better manage your interpersonal environment. Separate examination of behaviors and thoughts, connected to specific outcomes, can make complex and abstract life events simpler and more concrete.

Problems of Couples, Families, and Children

This part of the Appendix focuses on using Situational Analysis (SA) in more complex situations: as part of a family or couple. Often, our goals and behaviors do not exist totally independently, but are affected by others with whom we are close. For example, a married couple may have conflicting goals in situation after situation, causing them to frequently disagree and experience pain within the relationship. Parents may have little understanding of their desired outcomes (DOs) in stressful situations with their children, sometimes causing them to relate ambiguous messages and encourage acting-out behaviors that increase the tension in the household. Children themselves are generally not accustomed to examining their thoughts and behaviors in any systematic fashion. SA worksheets for each of these unique situations are presented herein, as are helpful case examples and transcripts.

COUPLES

If you have ever thought about or participated in therapy with your significant other, you may have been experiencing one or several of many different types of relationship difficulties, such as communication problems, infidelity, financial problems, or excessive arguments. Obstacles within romantic relationships can be very complex and are often remarkably difficult to unravel and improve. SA can be extremely helpful in analyzing these types of problems, either in therapy or on your own. As with other relationships, couples in romantic relationships may be unaware of the nonverbal messages that they communicate to each other or of the goals that they have in the relationship. With the help of SA, you can begin to examine your stressful interactions with your partner and learn to think and respond in ways that may increase the chances that both of you will achieve your DOs in these situations.

At the beginning of therapy with a couples counselor who is using SA to help you solve your relationship difficulties, he or she might explain the goals of therapy something like this:

> We are going to be working together over the next few months in an effort to solve some of the problems that have developed in your relationship. The core focus of this treatment is on the discrepancy between what you want to happen in a specific situation and what is actually happening. By examining the patterns of interaction between the two of you, we will begin to uncover ways in which you both can get what you want.

Your therapist will also explain that it is extremely important that both you and your significant other are committed to putting in the time and effort needed to successfully participate in this therapy.

As therapy proceeds, you will begin the actual SA process. Each of you should complete a SA worksheet about the same stressful situation independently, filling in your own description of the situation, as well as your thoughts and behaviors. In addition, you should be sure to identify your DO using the SUPERB guidelines outlined in chapter 5 of this workbook. The next step involves comparing your SA worksheet with your partner's, step-by-step. Couples often are surprised to learn that although they had similar goals in the situation, neither of them got what they wanted. Similarly, couples may have different goals that may complement each other. A third and more difficult possibility is that you and your significant other have DOs that conflict. It may prove extremely helpful for you to learn the things your partner wants from these situations and how these compare with what you want. Figure B.1 is a sample form that you can use in couples therapy; next we offer an example case and transcript of a couple's therapy session.

SA for Couples: Joe and Sue

Sue and Joe presented for therapy to improve the quality of their relationship. They both reported difficulty communicating with each other and feared that several important issues had come between them that threat-

Situational Analysis Worksheet for Couples

Name: ____

Date of Situational Event: ______________________________

Instructions: Select one stressful event between you and your partner that took place during the past week and describe it using the format below.
Please try to fill out **all** parts of the questionnaire.

---

1. Describe what happened:

2. Describe your interpretation(s) of what happened; what did this situation mean to you?

3. Describe what you did during the situation:
   a. Eye Contact -
   b. Body Posture -
   c. Gestures -
   d. Timing -
   e. Other behaviors -

   What did you say? How did you say it?

4. Describe how you wanted the event to come out for you (Desired Outcome):

5. Describe how the event came out for you (Actual Outcome):

Was the desired outcome achieved?
(to be discussed after going over each partner's individual goals in the situation)

How does your desired outcome compare with your partner's desired outcome in this situation?

FIG. B.1. Situational Analysis Worksheet for Couples. Figure adapted from McCullough (2000) by Kelly C. Cukrowicz and Jennifer A. Minnix.

ened the future of their marriage. Specifically, during a period of time when the couple was geographically separated due to employment situations, Joe had an affair with a coworker. He stated that he never meant for the relationship to go as far as it did and that he regretted it tremendously. He also stated that he would never cheat on Sue again and hoped she would be able to get past his betrayal. He felt that they argued much more now than they ever had before because she was angry with and embittered toward him.

Joe thought that Sue was resentful because she had to take a less satisfying job to be in the same place as him after he violated her trust. His goal for therapy was to increase their communication about his affair in a more constructive way so that they could move past it. He also wanted to regain her trust and their previous level of camaraderie and affection. Sue reported intense anger toward Joe because of his infidelity. She also had difficulty trusting him when he worked late, had to go out of town, or spoke of female coworkers. She said that any time these issues came up she felt insecure and upset, sometimes resulting in "neurotic" outbursts. She also stated that she had begun to question the foundation of their marriage and all of her faith in it and in Joe. Sue further stated that she hated the way she felt and the person that she had become. Her goal for therapy was to gain trust in Joe, gain a greater understanding of why he had been unfaithful to her, and to come to terms with her feelings so that she could move past them.

The following is a transcript of a SA exercise the couple completed in their fifth session, based on the two sample SA worksheets (see Figs. B.2 and B.3). At this point, the couple had completed several SA worksheets in therapy, and they were fairly comfortable with the method.

Therapist (T): I asked the two of you to each fill out a SA worksheet for an interaction you have had since we last met. Were you each able to do this?

Joe (J): Yes.

Sue (S): Yes. We agreed to write about an argument we had about Joe's affair.

T: OK. I would like to begin by asking each of you to read your SA worksheet to me. I would appreciate it if you could take turns without commenting on the other's worksheet initially. We will have time to discuss them together in a few minutes. Sue, why don't you go first? Read each part to us.

S: OK. Well, Joe and I were talking about our days after work on Wednesday. Joe mentioned that he had met with Debbie, his boss, about a project they are working on. I immediately began to wonder what was going on between them.

Sue's Situational Analysis Worksheet for Couples

Name: *Sue*

Date of Situational Event: *Wednesday, April 29, 2004*

Instructions: Select one stressful event between you and your partner that took place during the past week and describe it using the format below. Please try to fill out **all** parts of the questionnaire.

---

1. Describe what happened:
   Joe and I were discussing our day. He told me about a project he was working on with his female boss. I asked him if "project" meant affair. He rolled his eyes and I got angry and started screaming.

2. Describe your interpretation(s) of what happened; what did this situation mean to you?
   He doesn't love me. He is probably having another affair. I'll never be able to trust him.

3. Describe what you did during the situation:
   a. Eye Contact -
   b. Body Posture -
   c. Gestures -
   d. Timing - *left the room before he could talk*
   e. Other behaviors - *stormed out; crying*

   What did you say? How did you say it?
   Screamed "go away" from my bedroom

4. Describe how you wanted the event to come out for you (Desired Outcome):
   I wanted Joe to acknowledge my feelings and understand why I was upset - I wanted him to try and make me feel better

5. Describe how the event came out for you (Actual Outcome):
   I felt insecure, angry, & unconnected to Joe; we didn't resolve anything

Was the desired outcome achieved? *NO!!!*

(to be discussed after going over each partner's individual goals in the situation)

How does your desired outcome compare with your partner's desired outcome in this situation?

FIG. B.2. Sue's Situational Analysis Worksheet for Couples. Figure adapted from McCullough (2000) by Kelly C. Cukrowicz and Jennifer A. Minnix.

Situational Analysis Worksheet for Couples

Name: *Joe*

Date of Situational Event: *Wednesday, April 29, 2004*

Instructions: Select one stressful event between you and your partner that took place during the past week and describe it using the format below. Please try to fill out **all** parts of the questionnaire.

1. Describe what happened:
   I came home from work and tried to tell Sue about my meeting with my boss and the new project we were doing; she freaked out.

2. Describe your interpretation(s) of what happened; what did this situation mean to you?
   She will never get past this.
   She will never stop being suspicious about other women.
   I will always feel like a jerk.

3. Describe what you did during the situation:
   a. Eye Contact - *rolled my eyes*
   b. Body Posture -
   c. Gestures -
   d. Timing -
   e. Other behaviors -

   What did you say? How did you say it?
   Tried to tell her I loved her; told her she was wrong not to trust me

4. Describe how you wanted the event to come out for you (Desired Outcome):
   I wanted her to quit assuming the worst and I wanted her to listen to my story about my day. I really want her to just trust me.

5. Describe how the event came out for you (Actual Outcome):
   I felt guilty again & didn't get to tell her about the new project and how excited I was.

Was the desired outcome achieved? *Nope*
(to be discussed after going over each partner's individual goals in the situation)

How does your desired outcome compare with your partner's desired outcome in this situation?

FIG. B.3. Joe's Situational Analysis Worksheet for Couples. Figure adapted from McCullough (2000) by Kelly C. Cukrowicz and Jennifer A. Minnix.

So I asked Joe if "a project" was code for another affair. He rolled his eyes at me and told me that he thought I was overreacting as usual. I got even madder and started screaming at him about his affair and how much I blame him for how I feel. I started crying and stormed into our room. I locked the door and yelled at him to go away and leave me alone. I called my friend Mark and talked to him about it. My interpretations of the situation were that Joe was probably having another affair. That he doesn't love me. And that I am never going to be able to trust him. What I did was to ask Joe if he is having an affair with his boss. I yelled at him. I cried. And then I went to our room and locked him out.

What I wanted was for Joe to acknowledge that my feelings are warranted since he cheated on me before. I wanted to feel like Joe understood my reaction and wanted to make me feel better. My AO was that I ended up feeling paranoid, insecure, angry, and completely unconnected to Joe. Joe didn't say anything to make me feel better; he simply stated that I overreacted as usual. We didn't resolve anything in the end, either.

T: Sue, did you get what you wanted?

S: Absolutely not!

T: Thank you, Sue. Joe, why don't you read your SA worksheet for us so we can see how you experienced the situation.

J: I will, but I can tell you right away that Sue and I aren't on the same page here.

T: OK. I hope that we'll be able to make some progress with that by going through this. Does that sound OK to you?

J: Yeah. All right, here we go. I was trying to talk to Sue about my day when she freaked out on me. I mentioned a meeting I had with Debbie because it had been a good part of my day. Debbie was really happy with a new idea I had for a project we were working on. Anyway, Sue immediately assumes that I am cheating on her again and starts yelling and screaming and crying. I don't know why she does that. Why can't she believe me when I say it will never happen again? Why does every woman in my life have to be a threat to her? Well anyway, so after her outburst she went into our room and completely shut me out. I tried to tell her that I love her and won't ever cheat again, but she was too busy yelling at me about how awful I am to listen. After a few minutes I gave up and went into the living room to watch TV.

T: OK; now tell us what your interpretations of the situation were.

J: Well, last time you told us to think about what the situation meant to us. To me, it meant that she is never going to get past this. She will never stop freaking out at every little thing I do that involves a woman. And I will continue to feel like a jerk for the rest of our marriage. As for what I did: Like I said, I tried to tell her that she is wrong not to trust me and that I won't ever do it again.

T: Great. Now why don't you tell us what your DO was and what your AO was.

J: My DO was for her to listen to what I had to say about my meeting with Debbie without getting upset. I want her to trust me and quit assuming the worst. My AO was that I didn't ever get to tell her how happy I was to be able to contribute something important at work. I ended up feeling terrible about myself and angry and frustrated with her.

T: OK, did you get what you wanted?

J: No, not at all.

T: OK. This seems like a really good situation for the two of you to look at in therapy. First, let me say that you both did a great job filling out the SA worksheet. You agreed on a situation, you each filled out a worksheet, and you completed each part in exactly the way we talked about last time. Now, the first thing I want to talk about is some similarities I see. First, you both really want to get past this and to be able to trust each other again. Second, you both want to be able to understand each other and be understood. This is great. Now, on the downside, there are a couple of differences. Joe, you want Sue to be past this and she isn't. And Sue, you wanted Joe to acknowledge your feelings and you didn't think he had. These are good starting points for us.

J: I don't know. Honestly, it seems like those are impossible goals we have set.

S: Come on now. Why do you do that? Can't you have some hope? Why are you always looking at the bad side?

J: Me? Whatever! You are the one who assumed I was having an affair because I mentioned a meeting with Debbie. You're the one who always assumes the worst.

T: OK—let's stop here. I can see the two of you are feeling pretty emotional right now. Why don't we try to take a step back by talking through these SA worksheets each of you brought in? Sue, let's start with yours. If I understand you correctly, your DO in this situation was for Joe to acknowledge that your feelings were valid and for him to understand why you react the way you do when he mentions a woman. Does that sound about right?

S: Yes, it does. I just don't think that sounds like too much to ask.

T: OK. Let's start with your interpretations. As we have done before, I want you to tell me whether each interpretation you had helped you get your DO or hurt you. You said one interpretation you had was that Joe was probably having another affair. Did that interpretation help you or hurt you to get your DO of Joe acknowledging your feelings and understanding your reactions?

S: Well, I think it probably hurt me . . . though I don't see it as having much impact really. I guess it hurt me because my interpretation led me to react in a way that was very emotionally and not rational. He hates it when I get so emotional that we can't talk things out.

T: Can you think of another interpretation that might have helped you to get your DO?

S: Well, I could have tried to stop myself from thinking the worst by recognizing that he will always have women in his life and he can't possibly be having affairs with all of them.

T: Hmmm. If you'd had that thought, would you have gotten your DO?

S: Maybe. I probably would have felt pretty stupid for thinking he could have affairs with everyone. It is harder to feel stupid and recognize the error in my thinking when it is just one woman.

T: Let's look at the next interpretation you had. You said your second interpretation was that Joe doesn't love you. Did that interpretation help you or hurt you in getting your DO of Joe acknowledging your feelings and understanding your reactions?

S: Well, like the last one, my interpretation led me to get very emotional, which probably hurt me.

T: OK. Can you think of another interpretation that might have helped you get your DO?

S: I'm not really sure. Joe didn't know I was thinking that he didn't love me. So I am not sure what difference it would have made if I thought he did love me.

T: That is an interesting point you raise—that your DO rests on Joe's actions and feelings. We will get back to that. Let's look at your behaviors now. You said that you asked Joe if he is having an affair. Did that help you or hurt you to get your DO of Joe acknowledging your feelings and understanding your reactions?

S: I think it should have helped me. If Joe could put himself in my shoes he would be able to understand why I jump to those conclusions. I think it's best that I share those thoughts with him whenever I have them.

T: OK. So if I understand you correctly you are saying that you think asking Joe if he is having an affair helps you to get him to understand your feelings by illustrating them to him. Correct?

S: Yes.

T: Next, you said you yelled, cried, and locked yourself in your room. Did these behaviors help you or hurt you to get your DO?

S: They probably hurt me. Joe gets frustrated when I act this way, and I think that makes it less likely that he will try to see things my way. I also know that I yelled over him a few times. That probably made things worse.

T: What could you have done instead that would have helped you to get your DO of Joe understanding and acknowledging your feelings?

S: Well, I could have counted to ten to calm myself down, then asked him if we could sit down and talk about some of the thoughts I was having.

T: If you had done that would you have gotten your DO?

S: I'm not sure. It depends on Joe.

T: You're exactly right. That is a point I was hoping you would recognize. Tell me what that means to you, based on what you know about DOs.

S: I guess it means that I didn't really have any control. I can't make him understand me and relate to me in a specific way, as much as I want to. So what do I do when I find myself in this situation?

T: The first recommendation I would make is to try to think of a DO that is under your control and work toward that. It is unrealistic to work toward changing someone else's actions. We just can't do it. In this situation, what would have been a DO you could have had that would have been within your control?

S: Gosh, I'm not sure. I guess my DO could have been to keep my emotions under control and not freak out.

T: Good. I can see how some of the alternatives you mentioned earlier might have helped with that. You said you could have recognized that Joe couldn't possibly have affairs with everyone, you could have thought about how much you know Joe does love you, you could have counted to ten to gain control of yourself, and you could have asked Joe to sit down and talk with you. If you had done those things, would you have been able to keep your emotions under control and not freak out?

S: I think so.

T: Great! OK, now Joe. Let's talk through your SA worksheet. You said your DO was for Sue to listen to what you had to say about your meeting with Debbie without getting upset. I think this represents your larger DO that she will trust you and quit assuming the worst. Does that sound right?

J: Yes.

T: OK. Would you mind if we focus on Sue trusting you and not assuming the worst as your DO?

J: No. That's fine.

T: OK. Your first interpretation was that Sue is never going to get past this. Did that interpretation help you or hurt you in getting your DO of Sue trusting you and not assuming the worst?

J: I think it hurt me.

T: How so?

J: Well, if I assume she is never going to get past it then I probably won't do the things I should to help her get past it and begin to trust me.

T: OK, so what interpretation could you have had that might have helped you to get your DO of her trusting you?

J: I could have thought that it is normal for her to react the way she does. I did cheat, after all. It hasn't been that long, so it may not be realistic to expect her to have put it behind her.

T: These sound like good alternatives. If you had thought that this is a normal reaction, would that have helped you to get your DO of her trusting you?

J: No. She'll get there when she is ready. I can't force her to trust me.

T: How about the next one you said: that it hasn't been that long since you cheated on her and it may not be realistic for her to have put it behind her already.

J: I think the same thing about that one. It is like Sue's DO. I can't control her feelings.

T: It is good to recognize that. I want to talk about that more, but let's explore your interpretations and behaviors a bit more before we do. Another interpretation you had was that you will continue to feel like a jerk for the rest of your marriage. Did that interpretation help or hurt you in getting your DO of her trusting you?

J: They seem unrelated to me. My feeling like a jerk has no impact on her trust. It just makes me wish she could move in that direction more quickly.

T: Fair enough. As for your behaviors, you tried to tell her that she was wrong not to trust you and that you won't ever cheat again. Did that help you or hurt you get your DO?

J: It should have helped me. I was trying to tell her the sorts of things I thought would help repair her trust. But they didn't help.

T: Right. Why not?

J: Because it is up to her to determine when she can trust me. I know it is going to be a long healing process, and I can't rush it just because I feel lousy.

T: Great. Now, what DO could you have had that would have been in your control?

J: My DO could have been to listen to her even if it did seem like she was overreacting.

T: Let's go back through the alternatives you previously suggested to see what impact they would have had on that DO. You said you could have thought that it is normal for her to react the way she does. And that it hasn't been that long so it may not be realistic to expect her to have put it behind her. How do you think these interpretations would have affected your listening to her even if it did seem that she was overreacting?

J: Clearly they would have helped.

T: Now that we have gone through this together, what have you noticed about this situation?

S: I think both of us realize that we should be more careful about expecting things from each other. What do you think, Joe?

J: I tend to agree. You know I want us to get past this. It is just really hard sometimes, because I feel so responsible and I just hate that.

S: I know. And I hate it that I make that worse.

T: Can either of you tell me some ways you can generalize this to other situations in your relationship?

J: I can, actually. Another problem that we have is that I get bothered when Sue goes to her friends for support when we fight. I have always wished she would just calm down and talk to me. I can see now that I am probably somewhat to blame for that. When I act frustrated and impatient with her emotional reactions it just forces her to go elsewhere for support.

S: But I should try to use the strategies we've talked about for calming down and trying to think rationally too. I know that we never get anywhere when I shut you out. I always blame you for that, but I bear some responsibility too.

T: Excellent work. You guys are really mastering the fundamentals of this technique. The goal will be to continue to learn from the times when you don't quite make it to your DOs. We will also continue to talk about ways you can generalize from specific situations to global problems. That way you will be able to use these techniques later in your relationship and in other areas of your lives.

Summary and Conclusions

As you can see from this example, SA can effectively highlight thoughts and behaviors that can contribute to a couple's discontent in a structured manner. In the case of Joe and Sue, SA allowed them to see how their DOs compared to one another's, how they each contributed to the AO of the situation and, most important, how to apply what they learned to other stressful situations in their relationship. The structure of SA might be able to reduce the bickering that couples often engage in when trying to settle a dispute. Although the example of Sue and Joe included a therapist, you and your partner can use SA on your own, with plenty of practice and tips from this workbook.

FAMILIES

It is very common for parents to have conflicts with their children, and vice versa. Often, these are resolved with practice and patience. However, parents and children may find themselves in a pattern of arguing and fighting that you, as a parent, may feel helpless to control. This section applies SA to such situations. If both you and your children learn the SA method, you may develop a common format for discussing stressful interactions more effectively and master strategies that will allow you to get what you want. We present case examples from group therapy sessions in which parents work together to discuss and work through common problems they experience when disciplining their children. Children with diagnoses such as Attention-Deficit/Hyperactivity Disorder (AD/HD) or Oppositional Defiant Disorder (ODD), both of which can involve acting-out behaviors and defiant responding, are particularly difficult to discipline for many parents. Often, parents who try to discipline their children are in fact doing the opposite and are unwittingly reinforcing the very behaviors they wish to eliminate. Incorporating SA with established parent-training techniques (see chapter 6 of the companion text for a full description) can be very effective in teaching you, as a parent, to be very aware of your actions and goals in stressful situations with your children and to increase your chances of getting the outcomes that you want in these instances.

In this section we provide examples of SA worksheets that have been modified for adults and small children to learn. We also present examples of completed SA worksheets based on our experience with children with whom we have worked in our clinic. SA can be used effectively to teach social skills to children, both in a group setting and on an individual basis. Your child can learn to use SA to improve his or her success in situations at home or at school. This section describes many of the areas often covered with children in social skills training, such as being honest, reacting to failure, and accepting consequences. We have provided a list of many of the social skills that children are able to learn and use with the SA process (see Fig. B.4). When looking at this list, you may notice particular areas in which your child has weaknesses, as well as areas in which he or she has strength. This list can help you focus on the key weaknesses that may be keeping your child from getting what he or she wants in various situations. Although the SA technique initially encourages you to evaluate situations in hindsight and see what you should have done differently, the most important goal is for you (and your children) to learn to use this technique *during* stressful situations and to thereby increase your chances of getting what you want. The purpose of this section is to teach families to interact in ways that are meaningful, positive, and mutually beneficial and loving. Although you are encouraged to use these techniques on your own, we recommend working with a therapist, at least in the early stages. Let's start with a description and case example of how parents can use these methods in dealing with their own reactions to difficult situations with their children.

Situational Analysis for Parents

We have provided in Fig. B.5 a blank SA worksheet, modified for parents, which you can copy and use for your own situations. This section provides an example of a mother struggling to obtain her DOs in distressful situations with her young daughter. The case example is taken from a group therapy session in which parents collectively discuss their SA worksheets and aid each other in remediating thoughts and behaviors. Although we have found that group therapy applied to these problems seems beneficial to the parents with whom we have worked, you can use these methods on your own with the help of this workbook. We begin by describing this particular parent and the difficulties she reported when interacting with her child.

Skills Taught in Social Skills Therapy for Children

Introducing yourself

Beginning a conversation

Asking a question

Saying thank you

Ignoring distractions

Giving a compliment

Asking permission

Being honest

Sharing

Joining in

Dealing with boredom

Staying out of fights

Problem solving

Dealing with anger

Dealing with another's anger

Avoiding trouble

Accepting consequences

Dealing with group pressure

Saying no

Knowing your feelings

Expressing your feelings

Relaxing

Saying goodbye

Dealing with group pressure

Dealing with fear

Apologizing

Asking a favor

Reacting to failure

Dealing with losing

Ending a conversation

Deciding what caused a problem

Expressing affection

Accepting consequences

Negotiating

Smiling

Having fun

Dealing with fear

Responding to teasing

Accepting no

Suggesting an activity

FIG. B.4. Skills taught in social skills therapy for children (group or individual). Figure adapted from Kaduson & Schaeffer (2000).

Situational Analysis Worksheet for Parents

Name/s: ______________________________

Date of Situational Event: ______________________________

Instructions: Select one stressful event between you and your child/children that took place during the past week and describe it using the format below. Please try to fill out **all** parts of the questionnaire.

1. Describe what happened:

2. Describe your interpretation(s) of what happened; what did this situation mean to you?

3. Describe what you did during the situation:
   a. Eye Contact -
   b. Body Posture -
   c. Gestures -
   d. Timing -
   e. Other behaviors -

   What did you say? How did you say it?

4. Describe how you wanted the event to come out for you (Desired Outcome):

5. Describe how the event came out for you (Actual Outcome):

Was the desired outcome achieved?

FIG. B.5. Situational Analysis Worksheet for Parents. Figure adapted from McCullough (2000) by Rebecca R. Gerhardstein, Rita L. Ketterman, and Scharles C. Petty.

Case Example: Susan and Gretchen

Susan is a 39-year-old mother of three. Her daughter, Gretchen, is 10 years old and the middle child in her family. Gretchen's father lives with them at home but was not a part of treatment. Susan first brought Gretchen to the clinic because she wanted help with teaching Gretchen peer relation skills. Susan also wanted to reduce Gretchen's frequent emotional outbursts, which were beginning to interfere not only with Gretchen's relationships with her friends but also with her relationships at home. Gretchen received a diagnosis of ODD and was referred to the child group. Susan was not formally diagnosed, but it was clear from her interview that she was experiencing a depressed mood and chronic stress related to the problems that she was having with Gretchen. Susan was referred to the corresponding adult group.

Figure B.6 is a sample SA worksheet from a situation Susan shared with the group members about a problematic interaction with Gretchen. When discussing Susan's SA worksheet, the group decided to focus on Susan's DO of enforcing rules without yelling. It was determined that none of Susan's thoughts were helping her to calmly enforce her rules. Examples of some alternative thoughts were suggested, such as "If I give in to her this time, the next time I want Gretchen to do something she will be less likely to do it" and "Remain calm; yelling at Gretchen is not going to make her any more likely to go to bed." The group determined that both of these thoughts would likely help Susan to enforce her rules without yelling. In addition, the group decided that Susan's behavior of letting Gretchen stay up later was not helping Susan enforce her rules. Instead, it was suggested that Susan (a) escort Gretchen to her bed and turn off the lights; (b) remove distractions, such as television and video games; and (c) speak in a calm, no-nonsense voice telling (not asking) Gretchen that it is time for bed. Finally, Susan and the group were asked whether Susan would have been more likely to get what she wanted if she had used the alternative thoughts and behaviors. The group agreed that she probably would have gotten what she wanted using these helpful thoughts and actions.

Figure B.7 is a later SA worksheet completed by Susan about her daughter, Gretchen, in which Susan's DO was achieved. Throughout the course of treatment, Susan made a great deal of progress with her ability to evaluate her thoughts and behaviors. The sample worksheet represents the first time that she actually used the SA method while she was actively engaged in a situation. After weeks of considering the helpfulness of her thoughts and actions after the fact, she finally took the much-needed step and ap-

Susan's First Situational Analysis Worksheet for Parents

Name/s: *Susan*

Date of Situational Event: *Sunday, March 3, 2004*

Instructions: Select one stressful event between you and your child/children that took place during the past week and describe it using the format below. Please try to fill out **all** parts of the questionnaire.

---

1. Describe what happened:
   I asked Gretchen if she thought it was time for bed and we ended up getting into an argument about her bedtime. She was trying everything she could to get me to agree to let her stay up. I was getting angry and she was throwing a temper tantrum.

2. Describe your interpretation(s) of what happened; what did this situation mean to you?
   She knows exactly what to say to me to get me angry.
   I must be a very bad mother because I don't know how to get her to stop.
   Maybe I should just let her have it her way and enforce my rules next time.

3. Describe what you did during the situation:
   a. Eye Contact -
   b. Body Posture -
   c. Gestures -
   d. Timing -
   e. Other behaviors - *I gave in and gave her what she wanted*

   What did you say? How did you say it?
   I yelled at her for 30 minutes

4. Describe how you wanted the event to come out for you (Desired Outcome):
   I wanted Gretchen to stop yelling at me. I wanted her to go to bed on time like I had told her. I really wish I hadn't yelled at Gretchen and that I could enforce my rules without yelling.

5. Describe how the event came out for you (Actual Outcome):
   Gretchen stopped yelling, but she didn't go to bed on time. I didn't enforce my rules.

Was the desired outcome achieved? *NO!!*

FIG. B.6. Susan's First Situational Analysis Worksheet for Parents. Figure adapted from McCullough (2000) by Rebecca R. Gerhardstein, Rita L. Ketterman, and Scharles C. Petty.

Susan's Later Situational Analysis Worksheet for Parents

Name/s: *Susan*

Date of Situational Event: *Tuesday, April 28, 2004*

Instructions: Select one stressful event between you and your child/children that took place during the past week and describe it using the format below. Please try to fill out **all** parts of the questionnaire.

1. Describe what happened:
   Gretchen and I were driving in the car and she was really irritating me. She was being loud and kicking the back of my seat really hard. I told her to stop and she did not stop. I was getting more and more angry at her.

2. Describe your interpretation(s) of what happened; what did this situation mean to you?
   I thought she was being a complete brat.
   Wait, remember what we have talked about in group, you can control your own thoughts and behaviors. You know what to do.
   Relax, ignore her, she will stop.

3. Describe what you did during the situation:
   a. Eye Contact - *didn't look at her*
   b. Body Posture -
   c. Gestures - *stopped the car and turned the radio off*
   d. Timing -
   e. Other behaviors -

   What did you say? How did you say it?
   nothing

4. Describe how you wanted the event to come out for you (Desired Outcome):
   I really wanted Gretchen to stop kicking my seat, but I know that I couldn't completely control that. What I wanted for myself was to control my reaction to her (not yell, not swerve on the road).

5. Describe how the event came out for you (Actual Outcome):
   This was the first time that I actually got what I wanted. I controlled my reaction to my daughter. The really cool thing was that by controlling my reaction to Gretchen I impacted her behavior too (she stopped).

Was the desired outcome achieved? *Yes!!*

FIG. B.7. Susan's Later Situational Analysis Worksheet for Parents. Figure adapted from McCullough (2000) by Rebecca R. Gerhardstein, Rita L. Ketterman, and Scharles C. Petty.

plied the SA techniques during the situation. She excitedly brought this SA worksheet back to the group and was met with many accolades. Because of this reinforcement, she continued to use the SA technique for the remainder of the group sessions.

Conclusion

As this example shows, using SA can help you to clarify your goals during your interactions with your children, highlight the ways in which your behaviors and interpretations may be hurting you, and teach you to respond to difficult situations with your DO in mind. All of these increase your chances of getting what you want. This technique forces you to analyze your own contributions to situations and to identify patterns in responding that may be hurting you. As we describe next, the SA technique can also be used with children.

CHILDREN

Situational Analysis With Children

In this section we describe SA as it applies to the treatment of children. The SA worksheet presented in Fig. B.8 has been reformatted in line with the recommendations of Driscoll et al. (2004; see the companion text to this workbook) to accommodate children. The steps are described, and sample worksheets and case examples are provided. Each of these sections are discussed in greater detail in chapter 7 of the accompanying text.

Step 1: What Is the Problem?

In this step the child is asked to state the problem simply and concisely and to limit the detail to descriptive information only. To do this, the child should be encouraged to pretend that he or she is describing the situation as though it happened on a television program or in a movie he or she has seen. The benefit of this step, as in the adult SA worksheet, is that the child is forced to isolate problematic situations and to take an objective stance while describing them.

Situational Analysis Worksheet for Kids

Name: ______________________________

Date of Event: ______________________________

Instructions: Select one stressful event between you and your parents or friends that took place during the past week and describe it using the format below. Please try to fill out **all** parts of the questionnaire.

______ Family ______ School ______ Other

1. What is the problem?

2. Who or what caused the problem?

3. What does each person think or feel?

4. What are some plans?

5. What is the best plan?

6. Did the plan work?

7. What could you have done differently to prevent the problem?

FIG. B.8. Situational Analysis Worksheet for Kids. Figure created by Kimberly A. Driscoll and Karla K. Repper.

Step 2: Who or What Caused the Problem?

In Step 2, the child must identify the source of conflict. The kids' group in our clinic focused primarily on interpersonal conflicts, and Step 2 encourages the child to focus on the role that he or she and others play in conflicts.

Step 3: What Does Each Person Think or Feel?

Step 3 asks the child to consider his or her own thoughts and feelings, as well as the thoughts and feelings of others, to increase his or her awareness of how the feelings of others can affect the situation. For more advanced children, this step is sufficiently challenging to ensure sustained attention to the task.

Step 4: What Are Some Plans?

In Step 4 the child is asked to brainstorm about what he or she could have done in the situation. Asking the child what he or she actually did in the situation and writing his or her behavior down as a "plan" provides an opportunity in the next step to evaluate his or her actual actions during the situation. This step offers a nonjudgmental way to examine actions that could have been taken in the situation. In general, three or four plans provide ample material for evaluation in Step 5. Step 4 provides the child with an opportunity to creatively problem-solve without an emphasis on the "right answer": The therapist writes down all plans presented by the child, regardless of their viability or usefulness. The skills training component of the group helps the participating children build a repertoire of social tools to "plug into" this step of the SA worksheet, and we have found it helpful to encourage them to consider these skills when generating plans during the initial training of the SA process. If the child presents no appropriate behavioral plans, the therapist offers a brief suggestion for another possibility, preferably a previously taught social skill, to include in the list of plans.

Step 5: What Is the Best Plan?

Step 5 requires the child to choose the best plan from the list generated in Step 4. Doing this requires an evaluation of each of the possible plans. The cotherapists begin the evaluation of each plan by asking all the children in the group to think about what might happen if each plan were enacted and to label the plan as helpful or hurtful based on the predicted outcome. While working with the children to evaluate the plans, the cotherapists ask the group leading questions in an effort to guide the children to consider ways in which they could have used the previously learned social skills to prevent the original problem or to better the outcome of an already-problematic situation.

Step 6: Did the Plan Work?

In Step 6 the child is asked to consider specifically what he or she actually did in the situation and whether it worked out the way he or she wanted it to, as well as how his or her behavior was different from the "best plan" identified in the previous step. Although this step could be incorporated into Step 5, we believe that it is important to pay specific attention to the actual behaviors of the child in the situation and to isolate them for evaluation. Positioning this step after Steps 4 and 5, which are usually fun and hopeful, reduces some of the potential stress, embarrassment, or anger felt by the child while evaluating his or her own behavior (and having it evaluated by others). It has been our experience that, over time, children get used to this step and become increasingly able to objectively analyze their own behavior in relation to the outcome of the situation.

Step 7: What Could You Have Done Differently to Prevent the Problem?

Step 7 asks the child to think about ways to prevent the problem altogether. Unlike the first six steps of our modified SA worksheet, which focus on handling a problem once it arises, this step focuses on making good decisions *before* a problem arises. Many children who have social problems struggle with impulsivity, and this step is designed, in part, to address this issue.

Case Example: Anna

Anna is a 10-year-old girl in the fourth grade. Ms. Bloomington, Anna's mother, brought her to therapy because of minor oppositional behaviors in the home and decreased academic performance at school. She reported that Anna had become increasingly defiant over the past several months, and the behavior problems began at approximately the same time that Ms. Bloomington's boyfriend had moved into the family home. Anna was reportedly defiant, and she frequently sought negative attention by annoying others and arguing. In addition, she repeatedly lied and denied responsibility for her actions. Anna was diagnosed with Disruptive Behavior Disorder Not Otherwise Specified because she did not meet full diagnostic criteria for ODD. Her mother reported that she did not exhibit any serious psychiatric symptoms such as suicidal/homicidal ideations, hallucinations, delusions, or substance use. Ms. Bloomington admitted that her parenting style was probably more permissive than the typical parent. She indicated that she was interested in fostering a close, friendshiplike relationship with Anna and found it difficult to discipline her. In contrast, Ms. Bloomington's boyfriend demonstrated a more strict parenting style, demanding perfection and blind obedience. Ms. Bloomington and her boyfriend could not agree on a parenting style that fit both of their needs.

Figure B.9 is an example of a SA worksheet that Anna brought in to a therapy session, and the following is a transcript of the related discussion. The modified SA worksheet was used with Anna to decrease her lying and to increase the likelihood that she would take responsibility for her actions. In the following example, Anna accepted responsibility for her actions and successfully generated an appropriate alternative to the problematic behavior:

Therapist (T): So tell me Anna, what was the problem?

Anna (A): I got into trouble because I hit my cousin.

T: Who or what caused the problem?

A: Well, my cousin caused part of it because she said something mean to me, but I guess I caused part of it because I hit her.

T: What does each person think or feel?

A: My cousin feels hurt, and I feel bad about what I did.

T: What are some plans?

A: I could say "I'm sorry." I could have not hit her. I could not even worry about hitting her.

T: Can you think of some skills we've talked about before that remind you of this situation?

A: Staying out of fights?

T: Yeah—I think that's a good one here. Can you remember what the steps of this were?

A: Um, I think they were stopping and counting to ten, deciding what the problem is, thinking about choices like walking away, talking to my cousin in a friendly way, and asking my mother for help.

T: What do you suppose would have happened if you did that?

A: I probably would not have hit my cousin.

T: So, what do you think is the best plan?

Anna's Situational Analysis Worksheet for Kids

Name: *Anna*

Date of Event: *January 7, 2004*

Instructions: Select one stressful event between you and your parents or friends that took place during the past week and describe it using the format below. Please try to fill out **all** parts of the questionnaire.

__✓__ Family ______ School ______ Other

1. What is the problem?
I got in trouble because I hit my cousin.

2. Who or what caused the problem?
She did - my cousin

3. What does each person think or feel?
I feel sad because I got in trouble.
She feels hurt.

4. What are some plans?
To say sorry.
To not have hit her in the first place.
To not care that I hit her.

5. What is the best plan?
To not hit her.

6. Did the plan work?
No - I didn't use it.

7. What could you have done differently to prevent the problem?
Counted to 10
Walked away
Stay out of the fight

FIG. B.9. Anna's Situational Analysis Worksheet for Kids. Figure created by Kimberly A. Driscoll and Karla K. Repper.

A: Count to ten and don't hit her, then walk away.

T: What could you have done differently to prevent the problem?

A: I could have ignored what my cousin said to me and walked away so that I wouldn't have hit her.

T: Good job, Anna; I think you picked a good plan.

Anna quickly learned the social skills and the format of the modified SA worksheet. At the end of each session she was given several blank forms to complete as homework, and she usually completed them as instructed. On a few occasions she would fail to complete her homework; at these times, the SA worksheet would be completed in session. Anna clearly understood the format of the SA worksheet; however, she usually failed to use her skills during real-time situations. Interestingly, it is likely that Anna chose not to use the skills she was learning for several reasons. One of the more likely reasons was Anna's desire for attention from her mother's boyfriend. By misbehaving, Anna was guaranteed attention, albeit negative attention, from Ms. Bloomington's boyfriend. Unfortunately, Ms. Bloomington and Anna terminated therapy prematurely. Ms. Bloomington and her boyfriend ended their relationship and, according to Ms. Bloomington, Anna's behavior improved dramatically once the boyfriend moved out of the family home.

Conclusion

Children can learn the SA process with the same ultimate goal as adults: To increase the chances of getting what they want out of situations. Although the example we provided involves a child and therapist, you can teach your child the SA process on your own using this workbook. Children, like adults, can apply SA to a variety of situations, such as problems with peers, coaches, siblings, parents, or teachers. As the child practices analyzing past situations, he or she can learn to apply these methods proactively in future situations. Finally, the SA method may provide you and your child with a common method for talking about difficult situations, thereby improving your style of communication and your relationship overall.

Anxiety

This section focuses on using Situational Analysis (SA) for problems related to the experience of excessive anxiety. Anxiety comes in many forms and may affect your life in many different ways. Perhaps you are a generally anxious person, a worrier. Your friends, coworkers, and family may ask you why you're always so stressed out, why you can never relax, or why you're so high strung. Or perhaps you experience panic attacks that seem to strike out of nowhere, causing your heart to race, your chest to feel tight, and your palms to sweat, leaving you terrified that you may be having a heart attack or are going crazy. You may avoid public venues such as shopping malls or movie theatres for fear of having an attack and being unable to get away. Or perhaps it is only certain situations, such as social encounters or public speaking, that leave you panic stricken. You may avoid meeting new people, going to parties, expressing your opinions, or presenting your work for fear of rejection or ridicule.

Regardless of the sort of anxiety you experience, it is likely that there are several components to it: emotional, physical, and mental. Emotionally, you experience some form of fear, be it a constant, relatively low-grade worry or occasional bursts of pure terror. Physically, you experience certain sensations fundamental to anxiety, such as a pounding heart, shortness of breath, sweating, dizziness, muscle tension, or nausea, and mentally, you experience recurrent thought patterns focused on the likelihood that something terrible is going to happen.

The process of SA presented in this workbook offers a straightforward way to tackle these difficulties one discrete situation at a time. Although we recommend that you work with a therapist to derive the maximum benefit from these exercises, we have designed the materials presented here to provide you with some useful case examples and provide sample worksheets to assist you in practicing SA either with your therapist or on your own. These materials are divided into three sections targeting three different types of anxiety problems: (a) generalized anxiety, (b) panic attacks, and (c) social anxiety. Although there are similarities across these three types of anxiety, you will likely derive the most benefit from focusing on the section (or sections) that most closely resembles the difficulties you experience in your day-to-day life.

GENERALIZED ANXIETY

If you suffer from generalized anxiety, you are probably best described as a chronic worrier. You are constantly preoccupied with worry about any number of common life concerns, including your finances; your health; and the well-being of your family, your work, your home, and your relationships. This chronic worry may seem beyond your control. Your friends, family members, and coworkers may often tell you to "lighten up" and relax, or to quit being so concerned about the little things. You may have listened to them and tried to let go but found that the worries persisted, even when you tried to stop. Your worries may leave you feeling irritable, restless, and easily fatigued. You may experience muscle tension, difficulty concentrating on tasks, or sleep disturbances. These problems may be negatively affecting your work, your relationships, and even your health.

If you consult with a therapist about these difficulties (and again, it is strongly recommended that you do), he or she may teach you some techniques, such as relaxation strategies, for directly targeting the physical experience of anxiety. However, in addition to such exercises, you and your therapist can use SA to target the thoughts and behaviors that may be contributing to your experience of anxiety in specific situations. For example, you may not realize the extent to which your worries are exaggerated and unrealistic and how focusing on these distorted concerns may be preventing you from attaining your DOs for day-to-day events. Through SA you will learn to identify the thoughts and behaviors that are interfering with achievement of your goals by contributing to your anxiety and to replace them with more realistic, helpful thoughts and actions. You should realize that this will likely require you to put yourself in situations that would ordinarily cause you to worry—an undertaking that will probably be very challenging at first. However, with the help of your therapist and repeated practice with SA, you will soon discover that your worries are becoming much more controllable than you thought possible.

Case Example and Sample Worksheets

The main text of this workbook presents the steps of SA in detail, as they would apply to situations in general. Very little modification of this basic process is required in using this approach to the treatment of generalized anxiety. You will simply need to target situations in which you experienced problematic worry and pay close attention to the interpretations and behaviors (at Steps 2 and 3) that best encompass your experience of anxiety. Figure C.1 is a blank copy of the SA worksheet for generalized anxiety.

Now that you have familiarized yourself with the general framework, consider a case example of a person using SA in therapy to target her experience of generalized anxiety.

Maryanne is a 35-year-old lawyer and mother of two young children who came to therapy seeking help for excessive worry that she felt unable to control. She told her therapist that she had always been an anxious person but that in recent years she had been noticing that her fears were having an increasingly negative impact on her daily functioning. Maryanne reported that her primary worries centered around the safety of her children and her husband, but that she was constantly worried about something, including her job performance, her finances, her health, and her responsibilities at home. She said that she felt constantly on edge and that she was often irritable toward others, particularly her husband. Maryanne indicated that an example of her anxious behavior was her tendency to become extremely agitated if her husband was late coming home from work and to become convinced that he had gotten into a car accident or met with some other catastrophic fate. She noted that on such occasions she would place frantic calls to his office and to his cell phone until she managed to locate him and obtain reassurance of his safety. She further explained that she often tossed and turned in bed at night, worrying about unfinished tasks at work, bills that needed to be paid, or the possibility that one of her children might get sick. She expressed concerns that her anxiety was taking a toll on her marriage and on her job performance and noted that these concerns only served to increase her stress level.

Situational Analysis Worksheet for Generalized Anxiety

Name: ______________________________

Date of Situational Event: ______________________________

Situational Area: ______ Family ______ Work/School ______ Social

Instructions: Select one stressful event (in which you experienced anxiety or problematic worry) that happened to you during the past week and describe it using the format below. Please try to fill out **all** parts of the questionnaire.

1. Describe what happened:

2. Describe your interpretation(s) of what happened:

3. Describe what you did during the situation:

4. Describe how you wanted the event to come out for you (Desired Outcome):

5. Describe how the event came out for you (Actual Outcome):

RATE: Was the desired outcome achieved? Yes ____ No ____

FIG. C.1. Situational Analysis Worksheet for Generalized Anxiety. Figure adapted from McCullough (2000) by Ginette Blackhart, Sheila L. Stanley, and Andrea B. Burns.

Maryanne and her therapist agreed to use SA to target some of Maryanne's anxious thoughts and behaviors. After learning the basic process and reviewing some sample situations in session, Maryanne began to complete SA worksheets for homework between her therapy sessions. Figure C.2 is a sample worksheet completed by Maryanne for homework. A transcript of the conversation held between Maryanne and her therapist as they reviewed her homework in the next therapy session follows:

Therapist (T): So, Maryanne, I see you've brought in another SA worksheet for us to review. Why don't you tell me what happened?

Maryanne (M): Well, this is something that happened last weekend, and it's pretty typical of me. I'm always freaking out about stuff like this.

T: Then this should be a good one for us to review. Let's start with Step 1, and just tell me what happened.

M: Well, my husband took our two little girls to the zoo for the afternoon. I stayed home, because I had work to do. He told me they'd be home by around 4:00 pm, but by 4:30 they still hadn't come home. I started to freak out, and I called his cell phone a bunch of times, but he didn't answer. I wound up just pacing back and forth in the living room until they finally came home around 4:45. I was so upset by then that I just blew up at my husband for making me worry so much.

T: That's a great example of a situation that we can apply this method of SA to. It's a situation in which you got very worried and anxious, and it occurred in a discrete slice of time, lasting about 15 minutes. You also did a nice job in Step 1 of describing the situation from a fly on the wall perspective. Why don't we move on to Step 2? Tell me your interpretations of what was happening in that situation.

M: I was convinced that something terrible had happened to make them late, especially since I couldn't reach my husband on his cell phone. What I wrote down on this sheet was that I thought maybe they'd gotten in a car accident, or else one of the girls got hurt and my husband had to take her to the hospital.

T: OK, those are both thoughts that we can work with. How about Step 3? What were your behaviors in this situation?

M: I was really frightened, so I called my husband's cell phone a bunch of times, even though he wasn't answering. I also turned on the TV so if there were any reports of a major car accident I'd see it, and I just paced back and forth in the living room until they got home.

T: All right. You've done a really nice job of tracking your thoughts and your behaviors in this situation.

M: Yeah, like I said, I do this kind of thing a lot.

T: Okay then, let's take a look at the last two steps on the worksheet. What was your DO for this situation?

Maryanne's Situational Analysis Worksheet for Generalized Anxiety

Name: *Maryanne*

Date of Situational Event: *April 19th, 2004*

Situational Area: ✓ Family ____ Work/School ____ Social

Instructions: Select one stressful event (in which you experienced anxiety or problematic worry) that happened to you during the past week and describe it using the format below. Please try to fill out **all** parts of the questionnaire.

---

1. Describe what happened:
My husband took our two daughters to the zoo for the afternoon. He said they would come home by 4:00 pm, but by 4:30 they still hadn't come home, and when I called my husband's cell phone, he did not answer. I became extremely anxious and spent the next 15 minutes pacing back and forth in the living room until they finally got home, by which time I was so upset that I completely blew up at my husband for making me worry.

2. Describe your interpretation(s) of what happened:
- They got into an accident.
- One of the girls got hurt and they had to rush to the hospital.

3. Describe what you did during the situation:
- Tried my husband's cell phone about 15 times
- Turned on the TV looking for reports of car accidents on the news
- Paced the living room until they got home

4. Describe how you wanted the event to come out for you (Desired Outcome):
To know exactly where they were the whole time, so I wouldn't have to worry about them.

5. Describe how the event came out for you (Actual Outcome):
My family came home safe and sound. They were late because they stopped for ice cream cones on the way home, and my husband's cell phone was turned off. But I was so upset that I couldn't even ask if they had fun, and my husband was really frustrated with me.

RATE: Was the desired outcome achieved? Yes ____ No *X*

FIG. C.2. Maryanne's Situational Analysis Worksheet for Generalized Anxiety. Figure adapted from McCullough (2000) by Ginette Blackhart, Sheila L. Stanley, and Andrea B. Burns.

M: Well, what I put down here was what I really wanted at the time, which was to know exactly where they were at all times so I wouldn't have to worry about them.

T: It sounds like you're a little hesitant about that DO. Why is that?

M: Well, that is what I really want when I'm feeling that way, but I guess it's not exactly a realistic goal. I mean, I can't be with my family all the time, so I guess I should just try not to worry so much. But I really feel like I can't help it!

T: You've brought up a really important point, and I'm glad you caught that yourself. You're right that it's probably unrealistic to want to know exactly where your husband and kids are at every moment, all the time. So it sounds like you think a better goal would be to endure their absence without getting so anxious. Is that right?

M: Yes, I think so. But that's really hard to do when they're late!

T: I can certainly see where that would be true. But then again, that's our goal in here—to help you get through the day-to-day stuff, including when people are late, without getting so anxious that it has a really unpleasant effect on your life and your relationships. So why don't we revise that DO a bit, and change it to reflect your goal of not getting so anxious?

M: OK. I think that's a good idea. That's supposed to be my goal all the time anyway.

T: What was the AO of this situation for you?

M: My family got home safe and sound. It turned out that they were late because they'd stopped for ice cream on the way home, and by mistake my husband had turned his cell phone off. So they were fine, but I was so upset from being so worried about them that I couldn't even ask if they'd had fun or what they'd seen at the zoo. I just blew up at my husband for being late and making me worry, and he wound up getting frustrated with me for being so irritable and getting worried over nothing.

T: OK, then, let's move on to the remediation stage of SA. Let's take another look at those interpretations you listed in Step 2, starting with that first one: "They got in a car accident." In light of your new DO of not getting so anxious about them being late, do you think that interpretation was helpful or hurtful?

M: Oh, it was definitely hurtful! Thinking that just makes my heart stop and my anxiety shoot through the roof.

T: That makes sense to me. How about that other interpretation: "One of the girls got hurt . . ."? Was that one helpful or hurtful to you in avoiding getting so anxious?

M: That was obviously hurtful too, just like the first one. It's one of the worst things that could happen, and thinking about it gets me all worked up. But those are the first thoughts that come to mind!

T: Well then, let's take advantage of our time together here and see if we can generate some alternatives. What else could you have thought, or how else could you have interpreted that situation, that might have been more helpful in getting that DO of not feeling so anxious?

M: Well, I guess I could have thought something like, "He's been late before and he's always been fine," or "Maybe there's a lot of traffic," or "Maybe they stopped somewhere." After all, that did wind up being the reason!

T: And if you'd thought those kinds of things instead, do you think it would have helped you to get your DO?

M: Yeah, I think so. I might still have been worried, but maybe I wouldn't have focused all my energy on the worst case scenarios, and that would have helped me stay calmer.

T: Great! Now, how about the behaviors you listed in Step 3? Let's take a look at those. Calling your husband's cell phone over and over . . . was that helpful or hurtful to you in getting your DO?

M: Hmmm . . . that one is a little tough to figure out. I guess calling him once wouldn't have been hurtful, and it might have helped if I'd gotten through to him. But calling over and over, even though it was clear that he wasn't picking up probably was more hurtful. Each time he didn't answer I got more and more convinced that something awful had happened.

T: So maybe it wasn't calling at all that was hurtful, but calling so many times?

M: Yes, I think that's right. That probably didn't help me in the end; it just kept me focused on wondering what was happening.

T: How about your other behaviors? Checking the TV? Pacing the living room?

M: Definitely hurtful. Doing that just kept me ruminating about the worst possible explanations for what was happening.

T: So if you could revise those behaviors, what sorts of things might have been more helpful to you in terms of staying calm?

M: I think if I'd just distracted myself for awhile . . . not looked at the clock but just did some more work or read a book or something. Or maybe I could have called a friend and chatted for awhile to keep my mind off the time.

T: Those all sound like reasonable solutions. So, to recap, if your interpretations had been more along the lines of "Maybe there's traffic, maybe they stopped somewhere," and if instead of pacing and checking the TV for accident reports you'd done some work or called a friend, you might have had a better shot at reaching your DO of getting through that experience without getting so anxious?

M: Definitely. If they'd been hours and hours late, I'd still have worried, of course, but if I'd done those things differently I could have gotten through those 45 minutes without getting so overwhelmed. And it did all turn out fine in the end.

By the end of this therapy session, Maryanne had completed the analysis of this situation and had revised the thoughts and behaviors that were interfering with her goal of surviving the situation without excessive anxiety. It's important to notice that Maryanne had to make an important adjustment to her DO, to bring it in line with the SUPERB principles outlined in chapter 5 in this workbook. The DO she originally chose, that she would know her husband and children's whereabouts at all times, might indeed have lessened her anxiety for their safety were she able to conceive of a way to bring that about. However, she herself noted that this goal was likely unrealistic and that a healthier approach to the situation would entail her being able to encounter such situations of uncertainty without being overwhelmed by fear of the worst. Maryanne's revised SA worksheet, which incorporates the changes made in session with the help of her therapist, is presented in Fig. C.3.

Maryanne's situation is typical of people with generalized anxiety, in that she tended to generate catastrophic interpretations about situations when other, more realistic interpretations were available. You may find yourself coming up with similarly extreme thoughts about situations at work (e.g., "I'm going to get fired if I make one mistake") or with friends or family (e.g., "If we have a fight, our relationship is finished permanently"), or about money (e.g., "We'll never get our bills paid, and we'll be out in the street"), or other issues. As you saw in Maryanne's case, such interpretations can contribute to unnecessarily extreme anxiety, which can wreak havoc on all areas of your daily functioning. Through practice with SA, particularly with the aid of a qualified therapist, you can learn to challenge these interpretations, and the behaviors that accompany them, and to generate more effective solutions for encountering these situations when they arise.

PANIC ATTACKS

An anxiety experience much different from the chronic, low-grade worry of generalized anxiety is the repeated occurrence of sudden, unexpected panic attacks. Individuals who experience such attacks are hit out of the blue with an intense feeling of fear, accompanied by physical sensations such as heart palpitations, sweating, shaking, shortness of breath, nausea, and dizziness. The attacks are so terrifying and so out of the blue that the person often fears that he or she is having a heart attack or dying, or if not, then perhaps she or he is going crazy. People who experience recurrent panic attacks may become preoccupied with concern that they might have an attack, they might worry about the potential consequences should an attack strike (e.g., public embarrassment, losing control, suffering a heart attack), and they might substantially alter their behavior as a result of these concerns. Some people who experience panic attacks become so affected by the fear of having another attack in an inescapable situation that they

Maryanne's Revised Situational Analysis Worksheet for Generalized Anxiety

Name: *Maryanne*

Date of Situational Event: *April 19th, 2004*

Situational Area: ✓ Family ____ Work/School ____ Social

Instructions: Select one stressful event (in which you experienced anxiety or problematic worry) that happened to you during the past week and describe it using the format below. Please try to fill out **all** parts of the questionnaire.

1. Describe what happened:
My husband took our two daughters to the zoo for the afternoon. He said they would come home by 4:00 pm, but by 4:30 they still hadn't come home, and when I called my husband's cell phone, he did not answer. I became extremely anxious and spent the next 15 minutes pacing back and forth in the living room until they finally got home, by which time I was so upset that I completely blew up at my husband for making me worry.

2. Describe your interpretation(s) of what happened:
- ~~*They got into an accident.*~~
- ~~*One of the girls got hurt and they had to rush to the hospital.*~~
- *Maybe there was traffic, or they stopped somewhere on the way home.*

3. Describe what you did during the situation:
- *Tried my husband's cell phone ~~about 15 times~~ once*
- ~~*Turned on the TV looking for reports of car accidents on the news*~~
- ~~*Paced the living room until they got home*~~
- *Did some work or called a friend to chat for awhile*

4. Describe how you wanted the event to come out for you (Desired Outcome):
~~*To know exactly where they were the whole time, so I wouldn't have to worry about them.*~~
To get through the situation without getting too anxious.

5. Describe how the event came out for you (Actual Outcome):
My family came home safe and sound. They were late because they stopped for ice cream cones on the way home, and my husband's cell phone was turned off. But I was so upset that I couldn't even ask if they had fun, and my husband was really frustrated with me.

RATE: Was the desired outcome achieved? Yes ____ No *X*

FIG. C.3. Maryanne's Revised Situational Analysis Worksheet for Generalized Anxiety. Figure adapted from McCullough (2000) by Ginette Blackhart, Sheila L. Stanley, and Andrea B. Burns.

avoid certain places or situations (e.g., being away from home alone, being in a crowd, traveling by plane or bus) entirely.

If you go to a therapist for help in treating your panic attacks, you should be prepared for some challenging, even frightening, but ultimately effective activities. Your therapist will help you to overcome your panic attacks, but this is accomplished by forcing you to face your fears in a safe and controlled situation. Specifically, your therapist will give you exercises to do with the goal of deliberately inducing some of the symptoms of a panic attack in the therapy session. The primary reason for doing this is that inducing the symptoms of a panic attack in therapy provides an opportunity to notice and to challenge the interpretations and the behaviors that arise when a panic attack strikes. As described earlier, people who have experienced an unexpected panic attack may become extremely anxious over the possibility of having future attacks and the potential disastrous consequences of these attacks, to the point where they may even drastically alter their behavior to avoid situations they perceive to be dangerous. Paradoxically, however, this constant worry about the possibility of having a panic attack and the consequences that might follow can actually make it much *more* likely that future attacks will occur.

The process of SA provides one system that you and your therapist might use in conjunction with exercises in which you are deliberately exposed to feelings of panic in session. Furthermore, you may apply the SA framework to the analysis of situations outside of therapy in which you experienced panic. This method may prove helpful to you by requiring you to attend to the thoughts and behaviors that may actually be contributing to and exacerbating your experience of panic. It may also help you by giving you a context in which to generate alternative, more helpful interpretations and behaviors with the objective of preventing panic attacks in the future.

The basic process of SA presented in this workbook may be applied to the treatment of panic attacks with only one slight modification. A common component of the treatment of panic involves providing anxiety ratings on a 1-to-100 scale while anxiety is induced in session. In the companion text for this workbook, Driscoll et al. (2004) advocate including these ratings in the process of SA to highlight the manner in which feelings of anxiety and panic can follow directly from the interpretations one makes of situations. Accordingly, the worksheet for this application of SA includes this one slight alteration, in which an anxiety rating is required between Steps 2 and 3. Figure C.4 is a blank copy of the SA worksheet for panic attacks.

Situational Analysis Worksheet for Panic Attacks

Name: ______________________________

Date of Situational Event: ______________________________

Situational Area: ______ Family ______ Work/School ______ Social

---

Instructions: Select one situation from the past week in which you experienced feelings of panic and describe it using the format below.
Please try to fill out **all** parts of the questionnaire.

---

1. Describe what happened:

2. Describe your interpretation(s) of what happened:

   Rate your anxiety in this situation
   (1 to 100, with 100 being the worst anxiety imaginable):

3. Describe what you did during the situation:

4. Describe how you wanted the event to come out for you (Desired Outcome):

5. Describe how the event came out for you (Actual Outcome):

RATE: Was the desired outcome achieved? Yes ____ No ____

FIG. C.4. Situational Analysis Worksheet for Panic Attacks. Figure adapted from McCullough (2000) by Ginette Blackhart, Sheila L. Stanley, and Andrea B. Burns.

Case Example and Sample Worksheets

To better clarify the manner in which SA might be implemented in the treatment of panic attacks, consider the following case example. The material from this case is drawn in part from chapter 10 of the companion text for this workbook.

Kara is a 22-year-old college student who came to therapy seeking treatment for her recurrent panic attacks. She told her therapist that she had experienced her first panic attack at the age of 16 and that she had had two more attacks at the age of 19. She noted that her first panic attacks were probably caused by the drugs she had been using at the time. She had continued the use of drugs and alcohol for some time, and in the months before she entered therapy she had experienced more attacks, which seemed to be increasing in frequency. Suspecting her drug use was responsible, Kara stopped using drugs or alcohol altogether. However, her panic attacks persisted. By the time she began therapy, she was having at least two panic attacks per week.

Kara described her panic attacks as lasting anywhere from several minutes up to a maximum length of half an hour. During the attacks, her heart would race, she would have difficulty breathing, she would feel as though her throat were closing up, her stomach would feel twisted in knots, and she would worry that she was going crazy or that she was going to die. She told her therapist that although she was afraid of having attacks in hard-to-escape situations, she typically did not avoid driving, work, or social situations. However, she was afraid of having a panic attack while alone at home and would often spend the night at her friends' homes.

At the beginning of therapy, Kara's therapist taught her some basic relaxation techniques that were designed to help her manage her level of anxiety during a panic attack. They then began conducting exposure sessions in therapy, in which Kara would deliberately induce symptoms of panic (e.g., a pounding heart, hyperventilation) in session and would notice, with her therapist's help, the interpretations she made when those symptoms began. Kara and her therapist used the framework of SA to review those interpretations and to revise those that seemed to be contributing to her subjective experience of panic. Kara was also assigned to complete SA worksheets for homework between sessions, making note of any experiences of panic she had during the week.

The following is an example of a situation Kara selected for one of her homework assignments, which she reviewed with her therapist during a session. Her completed worksheet is presented in Fig. C.5.

Kara's Situational Analysis Worksheet for Panic Attacks

Name: *Kara*

Date of Situational Event: *June 15, 2004*

Situational Area: ______ Family ______ Work/School __✓__ Social

---

Instructions: Select one situation from the past week in which you experienced feelings of panic and describe it using the format below.
Please try to fill out **all** parts of the questionnaire.

---

1. Describe what happened:
   I went to the movies with a few friends and saw a new horror film. Partway through the movie, I started to get panicky. My heart was pounding, my head hurt, and I felt like I couldn't breathe. It was terrifying, and I had to leave the theatre.

2. Describe your interpretation(s) of what happened:
   - I'm going to die.
   - I'm totally out of control.

   Rate your anxiety in this situation
   (1 to 100, with 100 being the worst anxiety imaginable): *90*

3. Describe what you did during the situation:
   - I started hyperventilating.
   - I ran out of the theatre.

4. Describe how you wanted the event to come out for you (Desired Outcome):
   I just wanted to have a good time at the movies, without panicking.

5. Describe how the event came out for you (Actual Outcome):
   I was embarrassed that I made such a spectacle out of myself, and made my friends miss out on the end of the movie.

RATE: Was the desired outcome achieved? Yes _____ No __*X*__

FIG. C.5. Kara's Situational Analysis Worksheet for Panic Attacks. Figure adapted from McCullough (2000) by Ginette Blackhart, Sheila L. Stanley, and Andrea B. Burns.

Therapist (T): So, Kara, did you experience any panic symptoms or panic attacks since our last session?

Kara (K): Yes, I did, at the movies. It was awful! That's the situation I did my homework about this week.

T: All right, why don't we review it together? Let's begin with Step 1. Tell me what happened at the movies.

K: I went to the movies with some friends of mine. We went to see a new horror film that we were all really excited about. But partway through the movie I started to feel symptoms of panic coming on. My heart was pounding, I had a headache, and I felt like I couldn't breathe. I was absolutely terrified! I had to run out of the theatre and calm down out in the lobby.

T: Sounds like a perfect example of the sort of situation we're targeting with this exercise.

Having familiarized yourself with the steps of SA presented earlier in this book, you may notice that Kara's description of the situation at Step 1 seems to differ slightly from the descriptions usually sought. The descriptions of the situation typically are to take a fly on the wall perspective of what happened, which suggests an objective point of view. Kara's situation, however, does not appear to be fully objective, as it centers on her subjective experience of physical symptoms of panic. However, because it is these symptoms that are being specifically targeted for treatment, her description is appropriate. She still manages to keep her interpretations largely out of her account at this step, although she did acknowledge being terrified.

T: Let's take a look at Step 2, then. When you were in this situation, what were some of your interpretations of what was happening?

K: I was convinced that I was going to die. I also thought that I was totally out of control.

T: OK, so you felt out of control and thought you were going to die. How high did you rate your anxiety in this situation on a 1–100 scale?

K: It was really high. I put it at a 90.

T: Sounds like this was a pretty bad one. So we have our description of the situation, your interpretations of what was happening, and your anxiety rating. How about your behaviors? What did you put for Step 3?

K: I put that I started hyperventilating, and I ran out of the theatre.

T: All right. Let's take a look at the last two steps of the worksheet. What was your DO?

K: I just wanted to enjoy the movie, without having a panic attack.

T: What was the actual outcome of this situation for you?

K: I was really embarrassed that I made such a spectacle of myself. I also felt bad that I made my friends miss out on the movie, since they came after me when I ran out.

T: So did you get what you wanted out of this situation?

K: No, not at all! It was terrible!

T: It sounds like it was a really unpleasant experience for you. The good news is that by working with these situations the way we are, we should be able to help you to keep these attacks from affecting you this way in the future. Let's go ahead and switch to the remediation stage now. We're going to go back to the interpretations you mentioned at Step 2, and for each one we're going to ask the question "In light of your DO of enjoying the movie without having a panic attack, did that interpretation help you or hurt you?"

K: OK.

T: Let's start with your first interpretation: "I'm going to die." In light of your goal of not having a panic attack, do you think that interpretation helped you or hurt you?

K: I guess it hurt me.

T: Why?

K: Because thinking that I was going to die was a terrifying thought, and it probably just got me more scared than I otherwise was.

T: I can see how that might be. How about your second interpretation: "I'm out of control?" Was that one helpful or hurtful in light of your DO?

K: Hurtful. It's like the first one—it just gets me more panicked.

T: So if you could go back and have different interpretations of that situation, ones which might have been more helpful to you, what might some of those interpretations be?

K: Well, I guess I could have reminded myself that I've had panic attacks before and I've always survived. I could also have thought something like, "I can control this," since we've been practicing those relaxation techniques in here and I could have used them then. I could also have reminded myself that I was watching a really scary movie and that that might have been part of the reason why my heart was racing and all.

T: So if instead of thinking that you were out of control and likely to die, you had thought about how you've had panic attacks before and always survived, and told yourself that you have some tools available to help you control your panic symptoms, plus remembered that you were watching a scary movie that might have your system more aroused than usual, you might have been more likely to get your DO of avoiding a full-blown panic attack?

K: Well, I don't know for sure, but I bet the chances would have been better.

T: That's true, we can't know for sure. But it's something you could test out another time, should this sort of thing start to happen again, right?

K: Yes, I sure could.

T: So let's look at your behaviors now. That first behavior of hyperventilating . . . do you think that helped you or hurt you in getting your DO of avoiding a panic attack?

K: That definitely hurt. I should have done those breathing exercises you taught me instead, and it wouldn't have happened.

T: So if you had to do it over again, you might have tried implementing the relaxation techniques we've been practicing. Do you think that would have been more helpful?

K: Definitely.

T: And the last behavior: Running out of the theatre?

K: That was sort of helpful at the time, in that it got me out of the situation, but in the long run I think it was hurtful.

T: Remember, your DO was to enjoy the movie without panicking.

K: Yeah, so that was definitely hurtful. Neither I nor my friends got to enjoy the movie, because I ran out!

T: So if you could revise that behavior, what might you have done instead?

K: I could have kept reminding myself of my more helpful interpretations, and I could have practiced the relaxation techniques right there in my seat. At least I could have given it a decent try before I gave up and ran out.

By the end of this therapy session Kara identified and revised all of her problematic interpretations and behaviors that she and her therapist agreed were contributing to her experience of panic. As they noted in the session, it cannot be known for certain whether these alterations would have prevented the attack in question, but the alternatives they generated could (and should) be tested out in future situations, to determine whether, indeed, they help to achieve Kara's DO of not panicking. Kara's revised SA worksheet is depicted in Fig. C.6.

As Kara's case illustrates, the treatment of panic attacks can be challenging, because it requires you to endure, even to deliberately induce, feelings of panic so that you can learn new ways of understanding and interpreting those symptoms. Although it seems as though it would be far more pleasant to somehow magically ensure that those feelings never strike again, that may not be a realistic alternative. At some point in your life, for whatever reason, be it running up a flight of stairs, watching a scary movie, or feeling stress over an important interview, you are likely to experience those sensations of a pounding heart, a tightening chest, and so forth. The critical distinction between feeling those symptoms and having a full-blown panic attack lies in the interpretations you make when those symptoms begin and in the behaviors that follow. As was the case for generalized anxiety, catastrophic interpretations (e.g., "I'm having a heart attack!") tend to exacerbate those symptoms and elevate overall anxiety levels, thus making it more likely that future episodes of panic will occur. Using SA to identify and alter those problematic interpretations can help you immu-

Kara's Revised Situational Analysis Worksheet for Panic Attacks

Name: *Kara*

Date of Situational Event: *June 15, 2004*

Situational Area: ______ Family ______ Work/School __✓__ Social

---

Instructions: Select one situation from the past week in which you experienced feelings of panic and describe it using the format below.
Please try to fill out **all** parts of the questionnaire.

---

1. Describe what happened:
I went to the movies with a few friends and saw a new horror film. Partway through the movie, I started to get panicky. My heart was pounding, my head hurt, and I felt like I couldn't breathe. It was terrifying, and I had to leave the theatre.

2. Describe your interpretation(s) of what happened:
- ~~*I'm going to die.*~~
- ~~*I'm totally out of control.*~~
- *I've had panic attacks before and I've always survived.*
- *I do have control here—I can practice my relaxation techniques.*
- *I'm watching a scary movie, which may be contributing to my panic symptoms.*

Rate your anxiety in this situation
(1 to 100, with 100 being the worst anxiety imaginable): *90*

3. Describe what you did during the situation:
- ~~*I started hyperventilating.*~~
- ~~*I ran out of the theatre.*~~
- *Practice my breathing, other relaxation techniques*
- *Stay in my seat, try my best to get through it*
- *Keep reminding myself of helpful interpretations*

4. Describe how you wanted the event to come out for you (Desired Outcome):
I just wanted to have a good time at the movies, without panicking.

5. Describe how the event came out for you (Actual Outcome):
I was embarrassed that I made such a spectacle out of myself, and made my friends miss out on the end of the movie.

RATE: Was the desired outcome achieved? Yes _____ No __*X*__

FIG. C.6. Kara's Revised Situational Analysis Worksheet for Panic Attacks. Figure adapted from McCullough (2000) by Ginette Blackhart, Sheila L. Stanley, and Andrea B. Burns.

nize yourself against such dramatic and aversive experiences, as you learn to take greater control over both your mind and your body.

SOCIAL ANXIETY

Perhaps the most common type of anxiety, social anxiety is estimated to affect more than one in ten people in the course of their lifetime. People suffering from social anxiety are fearful of social or performance situations in which they are exposed to people they don't know and in which they may be evaluated by others. When placed in such a situation, these individuals almost immediately experience an intense anxiety response, which for some may closely resemble a panic attack (see the preceding section). People with social anxiety often report fears that they will embarrass themselves in some way or that others will think negatively of them. A common concern is that outward signs of anxiety, such as trembling or blushing, will be noticed and harshly judged. Although socially anxious individuals typically recognize that such intense fear is unreasonable and excessive, they often will avoid social and performance situations altogether—or, if they must be endured, they will endure them with dread. This intense anxiety can cause serious disruptions in one's ability to function socially and occupationally and in other areas of daily life.

As with the other anxiety conditions described in this part of the Appendix, if you seek treatment for social anxiety, you should be prepared to face your fears. Treatment may be conducted in groups, placing you in a situation with others who experience similar fears, so that each group member has the opportunity to interact with others in a safe, controlled environment. Alternatively, you may work individually with a therapist who will give you homework assignments involving placing yourself in social situations. Regardless of the specific approach, the goal will be to elicit feelings of social anxiety so that you might build an awareness of the interpretations you make and the behaviors you engage in when presented with a need for human interaction. SA provides you and your therapist with one useful framework for identifying, organizing, and remediating thought and action patterns that may inadvertently be contributing to your social anxiety.

Before beginning SA and social interaction exposure exercises, your therapist may teach you some basic relaxation techniques to help you to alleviate some of your anxiety when entering a feared situation. The basic process of SA for social anxiety is much the same as it is for any other type of problem, with a single slight modification. As was recommended for the treatment of panic attacks, the process of SA for the treatment of social anxiety incorporates an anxiety rating between Steps 2 and 3. By including this anxiety rating at this stage of SA, you will be able to see clearly the degree of anxiety you experienced in conjunction with a given set of interpretations and to note the extent to which different interpretations might have lessened your anxiety rating. A copy of the SA worksheet for social anxiety is presented in Fig. C.7.

Case Example and Sample Worksheets

To more clearly illustrate the manner in which SA may be applied to the treatment of social anxiety, consider the following case example. The material from this case was drawn in part from chapter 9 of the companion text for this workbook.

Fred is a 19-year-old college student who came to therapy seeking treatment for serious social anxiety. He reported that he had been somewhat socially anxious since the age of 12 but that his anxiety had become much more severe since he started college. Although Fred was able to participate in many solitary and family activities, he experienced profound anxiety in any situation in which he was forced to be around or interact with others. Anxiety-provoking situations included walking around his college campus; attending his classes; going to the mall, the grocery store, or the movies; eating in restaurants; going to parties; and having to speak to or in front of others. When placed in these types of situations, Fred's heart would pound, his palms would sweat, and he would feel sick to his stomach. He worried greatly about what others might be thinking of him or saying about him, and he believed that they were often evaluating him in a negative manner. Fred found it nearly impossible to make eye contact with others or to initiate or maintain a conversation. He had no friends or casual acquaintances at school, and he had never been on a date. Fred's family remained his only source of social support but, as they lived several hours from his college, he often felt quite lonely.

Fred and his therapist devised a treatment plan in which Fred would be given assignments to interact with others between therapy sessions. They then agreed to use SA to evaluate how those assignments had gone and what sorts of interpretations and behaviors Fred was making during them. A sample SA worksheet completed by Fred after one such assignment is presented in Fig. C.8. The following is a review of Fred's SA with his therapist in his next session:

Situational Analysis Worksheet for Social Anxiety

Name: ____

Date of Situational Event: ______________________________

Situational Area: ______ Family ______ Work/School ______ Social

Instructions: Select one social or performance situation from the past week in which you experienced feelings of anxiety and describe it using the format below. Please try to fill out **all** parts of the questionnaire.

1. Describe what happened:

2. Describe your interpretation(s) of what happened:

   Rate your anxiety in this situation
   (1 to 100, with 100 being the worst anxiety imaginable):

3. Describe what you did during the situation:

4. Describe how you wanted the event to come out for you (Desired Outcome):

5. Describe how the event came out for you (Actual Outcome):

RATE: Was the desired outcome achieved? Yes ____ No ____

FIG. C.7. Situational Analysis Worksheet for Social Anxiety. Adapted from McCullough (2000) by Bradley A. White, Kelly C. Cukrowicz, Ginette Blackhart, and Andrea B. Burns.

Fred's Situational Analysis Worksheet for Social Anxiety

Name: *Fred*

Date of Situational Event: *July 3, 2004*

Situational Area: _______ Family _______ Work/School ✓ Social

Instructions: Select one social or performance situation from the past week in which you experienced feelings of anxiety and describe it using the format below. Please try to fill out **all** parts of the questionnaire.

1. Describe what happened:
I went to the grocery store on Friday night. When I was in the checkout line, I said "hi" to the clerk and asked her how she was doing. She said she was fine. I couldn't think of anything else to say, so I didn't say anything else. Then I left the store.

2. Describe your interpretation(s) of what happened:
- I'm not normal because I'm here alone.
- She thinks I'm stupid because I have nothing to say.

Rate your anxiety in this situation
(1 to 100, with 100 being the worst anxiety imaginable): *85*

3. Describe what you did during the situation:
- When I said hi to the clerk I made eye contact with her.
- I kept my head down and looked at the floor the rest of the time.
- I spoke really softly.

4. Describe how you wanted the event to come out for you (Desired Outcome):
I wanted to get through the situation without getting anxious.

5. Describe how the event came out for you (Actual Outcome):
I completed my homework assignment and said "hi" to the clerk, but I felt really anxious and didn't have a conversation or talk to anyone else.

RATE: Was the desired outcome achieved? Yes _____ No *X*

FIG. C.8. Fred's Situational Analysis Worksheet for Social Anxiety. Adapted from McCullough (2000) by Bradley A. White, Kelly C. Cukrowicz, Ginette Blackhart, and Andrea B. Burns.

Therapist (T): Fred, the last time we met I gave you a homework assignment to have a social interaction with someone over the course of the week, and to complete an SA worksheet about that interaction. How did it go?

Fred (F): Well, I did it, but I don't think it went that well.

T: I'd like to hear all about it. Let's take a look at the SA worksheet you brought in, beginning with the first step. What happened when you went to complete your assignment?

F: I went to the grocery store on Friday night, and when I was in the checkout line I said "hi" to the clerk who was ringing up my groceries and asked her how she was doing. She said she was doing fine, but then I couldn't think of anything else to say, so I just took my groceries and left.

T: OK, on to Step 2. What were your interpretations of that situation?

F: I was thinking, "I'm not normal, because I'm here alone," and I was thinking that the clerk probably thought I was stupid because I couldn't think of anything to say.

T: All right, so your interpretations were that you're not normal because you're there alone, and the clerk thinks you're stupid because you had nothing to say. How anxious were you in that situation? What rating did you give yourself?

F: I gave it an 85. It was pretty bad, but not as bad as, like, having to give a speech in front of my class or anything.

T: So your anxiety was pretty high. Let's go on to Step 3. What were your behaviors in this situation?

F: Well, when I said "hi" to the clerk and asked how she was doing, I made eye contact with her, because that was part of my assignment. But the rest of the time I just kept my head down and looked at the floor. And when I said "hi" to her, I spoke really softly and sort of mumbled.

T: What was your DO for that situation? What goal were you shooting for?

F: I wanted to get through that conversation without feeling anxious.

T: And how did it all turn out? What was the actual outcome you put down at Step 5?

F: I did said "hi" to the clerk and she responded, but I was really anxious and couldn't think of anything else to say, so I just left.

T: So did you get what you wanted?

F: Well, no, obviously not. I felt really anxious the whole time.

The DO that Fred initially chose was to get through his homework assignment without experiencing any anxiety. After some consideration, however, he and his therapist agreed that this might not be a realistic goal, particularly as they were still in the earlier stages of treatment. Because the experience of some anxiety seemed certain, Fred elected to revise his DO to reflect completing his homework assignment while being able to tolerate the anxiety that was likely to accompany it.

T: So, did you get your revised DO?

F: Sort of. I did complete my homework assignment, but my anxiety was really high, and that bothered me a lot.

T: It sounds like you partially got your DO then, although the situation still might have gone better for you. Still, I want to take a second to commend you for getting through that homework assignment in light of how anxious it made you. That took a lot of guts.

F: It doesn't feel that way. I feel like a huge idiot.

T: Well let's see if we can learn anything from this situation. Let's go ahead into the remediation stage, and take a look at those interpretations you made back up at Step 2. The first one you listed was "I'm not normal, because I'm here alone." Do you think that interpretation helped you or hurt you in trying to get that DO of completing your homework while being able to tolerate your anxiety?

F: I think that was hurtful.

T: What was hurtful about it?

F: That thought made me not want to look at or talk to other people, because I figured they'd think the same thing. They'd think I was weird for being there alone and for talking to them. So worrying about all that just made me more anxious.

T: And that made it harder to tolerate your anxiety?

F: Yeah, it just made it worse I guess.

T: OK, how about your other interpretation? You wrote "She thinks I'm stupid because I have nothing to say." Was that interpretation helpful or hurtful in light of your DO?

F: Hurtful. It made me more anxious too.

T: So if you could revise those interpretations and make them more helpful to you in attaining your DO of getting through that assignment while being able to tolerate your anxiety, how might you do that?

F: Well, I could have told myself that it's normal to go to the grocery store alone—half the people in there were there alone.

T: OK, and what about the other one?

F: I could have thought that it's no big deal, and the clerk doesn't think I'm stupid. She probably didn't even notice.

T: So if your interpretations had been that going to the grocery store alone is normal and that the clerk didn't think you were stupid, do you think that would have improved your chances of getting your DO?

F: It probably would have. If I'd told myself that, then I probably wouldn't have been quite so anxious, and I might have even been able to come up with something else to say.

T: Well, speaking of doing things differently, let's take a look at the behaviors you listed in Step 3. Your first behavior was that when you spoke to the clerk, you made eye contact with her. Do you think that behavior was helpful or hurtful to you in getting your DO?

F: I think that was helpful. I mean, it was part of the assignment, and completing my assignment was part of my DO, so it helped that I did that.

T: Makes sense to me. How about the next one: The rest of the time, you kept your head down and looked at the floor. Was that helpful or hurtful in getting your DO?

F: That one was hurtful. If I'd been looking up, I might have made eye contact with other people and even said "hi." Plus, when I was looking at the ground I was just thinking about how I wasn't normal and I really wanted to leave.

T: So looking at the ground actually made you think more negatively?

F: Yes, I think so. If I'd had my head up and had looked at other people, I might have been distracted from those thoughts.

T: OK, so if you could revise that behavior, what might have been more helpful to you?

F: Keeping my head up and not looking at the floor.

T: All right, and how about that last behavior? When you spoke to the clerk, you spoke really softly and sort of mumbled. Do you think that behavior helped you or hurt you in getting your DO?

F: I think I did that because I was so sure she'd think I was stupid, so I guess it wasn't helpful.

T: What might have been more helpful?

F: Just saying "Hi, how're you doing?" in a normal voice. Maybe smiling too.

T: So, let me recap this situation. If your interpretations had been that it's normal to be at the grocery store alone and the clerk didn't think you were stupid, and if your behaviors had included making eye contact when you spoke to the clerk, keeping your head up the whole time you were in the store, and speaking in a normal voice, maybe even smiling, do you think you'd have had a better shot at getting your DO?

F: Yeah, I think so. It would still have been hard for me to do, but I think it might not have been quite as bad as it was.

With the help of his therapist, Fred was able to recognize that, in light of his experience of severe social anxiety, a DO of avoiding anxiety altogether was probably unrealistic in a forced social encounter such as the one he was assigned to complete. However, a DO that accepted the likelihood of anxiety but strove to minimize and tolerate it while still engaging socially was much more in line with the SUPERB principles outlined earlier in this workbook. With that new goal in mind, Fred was able to recognize the extent to which his pessimistic, self-blaming interpretations were preventing him from achieving his objectives. His revised SA worksheet is presented in Fig. C.9.

Fred's Revised Situational Analysis Worksheet for Social Anxiety

Name: *Fred*

Date of Situational Event: *July 3, 2004*

Situational Area: ______ Family ______ Work/School __✓__ Social

---

Instructions: Select one social or performance situation from the past week in which you experienced feelings of anxiety and describe it using the format below. Please try to fill out **all** parts of the questionnaire.

---

1. Describe what happened:
I went to the grocery store on Friday night. When I was in the checkout line, I said "hi" to the clerk and asked her how she was doing. She said she was fine. I couldn't think of anything else to say, so I didn't say anything else. Then I left the store.

2. Describe your interpretation(s) of what happened:
- ~~*I'm not normal because I'm here alone.*~~
- ~~*She thinks I'm stupid because I have nothing to say.*~~
- *It's normal to go to the store alone.*
- *It's no big deal, the clerk doesn't think I'm stupid.*

Rate your anxiety in this situation
(1 to 100, with 100 being the worst anxiety imaginable): *85*

3. Describe what you did during the situation:
- *When I said "hi" to the clerk I made eye contact with her.*
- ~~*I kept my head down and looked at the floor the rest of the time.*~~
- ~~*I spoke really softly.*~~
- *Keep my head up the whole time*
- *Speak at a normal volume and smile*

4. Describe how you wanted the event to come out for you (Desired Outcome):
~~*I wanted to get through the situation without getting anxious.*~~
Complete my homework assignment while tolerating my anxiety.

5. Describe how the event came out for you (Actual Outcome):
I completed my homework assignment and said hi to the clerk, but I felt really anxious and didn't have a conversation or talk to anyone else.

RATE: Was the desired outcome achieved? Yes _____ No __*X*__

FIG. C.9. Fred's Revised Situational Analysis Worksheet for Social Anxiety. Adapted from McCullough (2000) by Bradley A. White, Kelly C. Cukrowicz, Ginette Blackhart, and Andrea B. Burns.

Summary and Conclusions

As you have seen from the examples presented in this part of the Appendix, anxiety comes in many forms and can cause problems in multiple areas of people's lives. Although it is still ultimately unknown why some people suffer from debilitating anxiety and others do not, what is known is that deliberately eliciting and then challenging the interpretations and behaviors that accompany anxiety through methods such as SA can help people overcome the fears that have paralyzed them in the past. Learning to recognize that the interpretations you make of situations have a profound impact on your emotional experiences in those situations and on your subsequent behaviors allows you to begin to question those interpretations and to determine whether they might be interfering with your attainment of your own personal goals. Whether used in the context of therapy, as recommended, or on your own, we hope that this system will afford you some insight into the specific ways in which you might intervene with your anxious symptoms.

Anger Management and Correctional Settings

ANGER MANAGEMENT

If you are reading these materials, it is likely that things are not going as well for you as you might like. Loved ones, friends, or coworkers might have hinted or insisted that you have a problem with anger and suggested that you get help, or perhaps you yourself recognize that you have a problem with anger. Maybe your anger has led to conflicts with friends and family, has gotten you fired from jobs, or perhaps has even led to legal problems or trouble with the police. Although anger is a natural emotion that should not be bottled up or ignored, it can, at times, be expressed in ways that are harmful to you and to others.

People may have previously told you to "get control of yourself," "stop blowing up," and "just calm down." However, as you know, it is not that easy to stop a long-term habit of responding to provocative situations with anger. The good news is that with some hard work and persistence, you can begin to affect your anger and how you express it. If you are reading this workbook, it is likely that you are taking the first necessary steps to making such a change.

SA will help you examine interpersonal interactions in your life that lead to anger, one situation at a time. At first, you will begin to learn what thoughts and behaviors contribute to your anger in individual situations. With time, you will learn to change these habitual patterns of responding. As interpersonal situations in your life begin to proceed more smoothly, your confidence in your ability to control and express your anger will increase.

One of the unique things about Situational Analysis (SA) is that it uses a nonconfrontational approach to the treatment of anger. That means SA does not label your thoughts, behavior, reactions, or even your anger, as good or bad. Rather, it helps you focus on your goals in situations and to discover how you can begin to attain those goals. Then you alter your thoughts and behaviors to get what you want in situations.

You have probably noticed that many interpersonal interactions in your life haven't gone as you would have liked them to. For example, you may have wanted to convey a thought or feeling and hoped the person you were speaking with would understand you, but somehow something went wrong. You may have ended up blowing up at the person in frustration. SA is designed to get you to stand back and identify your goals in a given situation and to determine how to alter your thoughts and behaviors so you can increase your chances of acquiring your desired outcome (DO).

Although you can practice SA without the aid of a therapist, it is recommended that you work with a mental health professional (e.g., psychologist) when you begin practicing this technique. This is because having an objective point of view can help to keep you motivated and on track with your SAs. You and your therapist can determine, over time, when you can begin to work more independently. This will likely occur once you get the hang of SA and begin to reliably achieve your DOs. However, you should know that the therapist is not there to judge or confront you; rather, he or she is a collaborator who is interested in helping you get what you want out of situations.

Worksheet, Example, and Exercise

The main text of this patient workbook contains detailed information about how to use SA correctly in the course of your anger management treatment. It provides information about the therapeutic usefulness of each step alone and in conjunction with all of the steps. This part of the Appendix provides a sample worksheet, a case example, and a completed exercise that are specific to anger management problems.

Sample Worksheet

Let's start with a blank SA worksheet, presented in Fig. D.1, that you can photocopy to use for yourself in your work alone or with your therapist. This worksheet is similar to the original worksheet, with the exceptions (a)

Situational Analysis Worksheet for Anger Management

Name: ____

Date of Situational Event: ________________________________

Situational Area: ______ Family ______ Work/School ______ Social

Instructions: Select one stressful event (in which you experienced anger) that has happened to you during the past week and describe it using the format below. Please try to fill out **all** parts of the questionnaire.

1. Describe what happened:

2. Describe your interpretation(s) of what happened:

   2a. List how each of these interpretations made you feel:

3. Describe what you did during the situation:

4. Describe how you wanted the event to come out for you (Desired Outcome):

5. Describe how the event came out for you (Actual Outcome):

RATE: Was the desired outcome achieved? Yes ____ No ____

FIG. D.1. Situational Analysis Worksheet for Anger Management. Adapted from McCullough (2000) by Bradley A. White, Lorraine R. Reitzel, and Andrea B. Burns.

that the instructions now ask you to select an event in which you felt yourself getting angry and (b) the addition of the emotion, or feeling, component as recommended in Driscoll et al. (2004).

Case Example With Completed Exercise

Now that you've had a chance to look at a blank SA worksheet, let's consider a case example. Tyrone is a 35-year-old African American man who lives with his wife, Jamie, and three children: Terence (18), Dominique (15), and Clarise (12). He came to therapy at the urging of his wife, after the frequency of his fighting with his children escalated to the point where he had physically knocked down Terence during an argument. Tyrone admitted that he had a problem with anger but felt that he was just trying to be a firm parent to children who were gradually getting out of control. He also believed that the children were trying to play him and his wife against each other. For example, they would ask one parent for something, and if they were denied, they would then ask the other parent. This type of behavior would often result in subsequent conflicts with his wife. Tyrone was diagnosed as having relational problems with family members. The following is an example from the third session in therapy with Tyrone using SA:

Therapist (T): OK, Tyrone, so I see you have a situation for our SA today. Let's hear it.

Tyrone (Ty): OK. Clarise asked if her friend could spend the night with her at our house. I told her "no." She asked me why, and I said that there was no need for her friend to sleep over and that what goes on in this family was none of her friend's business. Clarise then went and asked her mother, who told her that her friend could sleep over. When Clarise arrived back at the house with her friend, I sent her friend right out of the house and told Clarise she was grounded for 2 weeks. She told me she hated me and ran upstairs.

T: That's a good example of a situation we can look at. It is an interpersonal event, it made you angry, it occurred during a specific slice of time, and you have explained it objectively, like a fly on the wall would see it. Tell me your DO.

Ty: I wanted Clarise to obey me without complaining or asking her mom after I've said "no."

T: What was the actual outcome (AO)?

Ty: Clarise asked her mother behind my back and disobeyed me.

T: So, did you get what you wanted in the situation?

Ty: No.

T: OK. Let's go to Step 2 and look at some of your interpretations of the situations. What were your thoughts as the situation was happening?

Ty: Well, I have . . . I can't stand it when that girl doesn't listen to me. I have the right to tell her what to do when she is living under my roof, and I can't believe she asked her mother behind my back again!

T: Those are good thoughts that we can work with. How did having each of those thoughts make you feel?

Ty: Angry. All of them just infuriated me. She knows I can't stand it when she does those things!

T: So, on a scale of 1 to 10, with 1 being a little anger and 10 being extreme anger, how angry did each thought make you? Write these down.

Ty: Okay, well I guess the first was a 9, the second a 7, and the third a 9.

T: Okay, what behaviors do you have down?

Ty: I could only think of two . . . I balled up my fist and talked in a loud tone.

T: You've been a good observer of your behavior. Let's move on to the remediation phase.

Astute readers will notice that the therapist in this example went out of sequence when asking about the steps in SA. In fact, she jumped from Step 1 (description of the situation) to Step 4 (DO) and then Step 5 (AO). When reviewing your SA with you, your therapist may choose to follow the steps in order, or he or she may choose to use the order that the therapist in this example did. In this case, the therapist went out of order so as to establish the disparity between the DO and the AO immediately, making it quite notable to Tyrone. When his attention is called to this fact early, the stage was set for him to consider how his thoughts, feelings, and behaviors may have contributed to the discrepancy between his DO and AO.

At this point, all information during the initial stage of the SA process has been completed: All five steps of the SA have been reviewed and clarified. Figure D.2 is an example of what Tyrone's SA worksheet would look like.

The next step of therapy entails the remediation phase of SA. As discussed in great detail in this workbook, this phase begins by reviewing the interpretations and behaviors (verbal and nonverbal) as being helpful or hurtful to attaining the specified DO. Here's the session excerpt:

T: Now let's look at each thought and behavior and see whether each was helpful or hurtful in reaching your DO of getting Clarise to obey you without complaining. Let's turn our attention to your thoughts now. Take the first thought: "I can't stand it when that girl doesn't listen to me!" What do you think?

Ty: Well, I am having a hard time seeing if it is really helpful or hurtful.

Tyrone's Situational Analysis Worksheet for Anger Management

Name: *Tyrone*

Date of Situational Event: *Monday, April 21, 2004*

Situational Area: ✓ Family ____ Work/School ____ Social

Instructions: Select one stressful event (in which you experienced anger) that has happened to you during the past week and describe it using the format below. Please try to fill out **all** parts of the questionnaire.

---

1. Describe what happened:
   Clarise asked if her friend could spend the night with her at our house. I told her "no." She asked me why and I said that there was no need for her friend to sleep over and that what goes on in this family was none of her friend's business. Clarise then went and asked her mother, who told her that her friend could sleep over. When Clarise arrived back at the house with her friend, I sent her friend right out of the house and told Clarise she was grounded for 2 weeks. She told me she hated me and ran upstairs.

2. Describe your interpretation(s) of what happened:
   a. *I can't stand it when that girl doesn't listen to me!*
   b. *I have the right to tell her what to do when she is living under my roof.*
   c. *I can't believe she asked her mother behind my back again!*

   2a. List how each of these interpretations made you feel:
   All made me feel angry. On a scale of 1–10 (10 = extreme anger); a. = 9, b. = 7, c. = 9.

3. Describe what you did during the situation:
   a. *Balled up my fists*
   b. *Talked in a loud tone*

4. Describe how you wanted the event to come out for you (Desired Outcome):
   I wanted Clarise to obey me without complaining.

5. Describe how the event came out for you (Actual Outcome):
   Clarise asked her mother behind my back and disobeyed me.

RATE: Was the desired outcome achieved? Yes ____ No ✓

FIG. D.2. Tyrone's Situational Analysis Worksheet for Anger Management. Adapted from McCullough (2000) by Bradley A. White, Lorraine R. Reitzel, and Andrea B. Burns.

T: OK, so you don't know if having the thought "I can't stand it when that girl doesn't listen to me!" is helpful or hurtful to getting Clarise to obey you without complaining. . . . I wonder if that means there is something wrong with your DO? Based on the workbook chapter you read about DOs, do you think that your outcome is a good one?

Ty: Oh yeah, the magic wand and all that. Well, I was still kind of mad when I filled this thing out. I knew you would say something about it being focused on someone else's behavior, too.

T: Well, you were right. DOs work best if they are focused on what you can control—your behaviors. Now that you're thinking about it, what was really your DO in the situation?

Ty: I wanted to tell Clarise her friend could not come over without upsetting her.

T: That sounds like a good one. Write that down. So did having the thought "I can't stand it when that girl doesn't listen to me!" help you or hurt you in attaining your DO of telling Clarise her friend could not come over without upsetting her?

Ty: Hurt me; it made me angry from the get-go.

T: OK, how about your next thought . . . "I have the right to tell her what to do when she is living under my roof!" Was that helpful or hurtful to telling Clarise her friend could not come over without upsetting her?

Ty: It was definitely hurtful as far as not upsetting her. I've said that to her before, and she usually gets pretty mad herself. Even though it's hurtful, I still think it's true, though.

T: Well, that may be, but we're really just interested in achieving your goal here and seeing if that thought is helping or hurting. If it's hurtful, we need to make a note of that. (*Tyrone nods.*) How about your last thought of, "I can't believe she asked her mother behind my back again!" Was that helpful or hurtful to getting your DO of telling Clarise her friend could not come over without upsetting her?

Ty: Well, again, it really just made me mad, which didn't make me feel like being nice to Clarise at the time. So, I guess hurtful.

T: Okay, now let's look at the behaviors you mentioned . . . balling up your fists and talking in a loud tone . . . were those behaviors helpful or hurtful to getting your DO of telling Clarise that her friend could not come over without upsetting her?

Ty: Oh. Those were definitely hurtful. Clarise does get upset when I yell at her, and I know she knew what to expect from me just by the tone of my voice. I guess I overreacted.

At this point, Tyrone should have written whether his interpretations and behaviors were helpful or hurtful on the SA worksheet. Also, he would have altered his DO to reflect the magic wand and SUPERB principles outlined in chapter 5. It should look something like the form presented in Fig. D.3, on which the most recent changes are indicated in boldface type.

Tyrone's First Revised Situational Analysis Worksheet for Anger Management

Name: *Tyrone*

Date of Situational Event: *Monday, April 21, 2004*

Situational Area: ✓ Family ____ Work/School ____ Social

Instructions: Select one stressful event (in which you experienced anger) that has happened to you during the past week and describe it using the format below. Please try to fill out **all** parts of the questionnaire.

---

1. Describe what happened:
Clarise asked if her friend could spend the night with her at our house. I told her "no." She asked me why and I said that there was no need for her friend to sleep over and that what goes on in this family was none of her friend's business. Clarise then went and asked her mother, who told her that her friend could sleep over. When Clarise arrived back at the house with her friend, I sent her friend right out of the house and told Clarise she was grounded for 2 weeks. She told me she hated me and ran upstairs.

2. Describe your interpretation(s) of what happened:
   a. *I can't stand it when that girl doesn't listen to me!* ***(Hurtful)***
   b. *I have the right to tell her what to do when she is living under my roof.* ***(Hurtful)***
   c. *I can't believe she asked her mother behind my back again!* ***(Hurtful)***

   2a. List how each of these interpretations made you feel:
   All made me feel angry. On a scale of 1–10 (10 = extreme anger); a. = 9, b. = 7, c. = 9.

3. Describe what you did during the situation:
   a. *Balled up my fists* ***(Hurtful)***
   b. *Talked in a loud tone* ***(Hurtful)***

4. Describe how you wanted the event to come out for you (Desired Outcome):
~~*I wanted Clarise to obey me without complaining.*~~ *I wanted to tell Clarise her friend could not come over without upsetting her.*

5. Describe how the event came out for you (Actual Outcome):
Clarise asked her mother behind my back and disobeyed me.

RATE: Was the desired outcome achieved? Yes ____ No ✓

FIG. D.3. Tyrone's First Revised Situational Analysis Worksheet for Anger Management. Adapted from McCullough (2000) by Bradley A. White, Lorraine R. Reitzel, and Andrea B. Burns.

The next step of the remediation phase entails changing your interpretations and behaviors so as to increase the chances of obtaining the DO.

T: OK, so we've established that you had some thoughts and behaviors in this situation that were overall not helpful in getting you to achieve your overall DO of telling Clarise her friend could not come over without upsetting her. How could we change the first thought of "I can't stand it when that girl doesn't listen to me!" so that it would increase the chances of you getting what you wanted out of the situation?

Ty: Well, I suppose I could have thought that Clarise would be more likely to listen to me if I don't overreact and jump down her throat.

T: OK, that sounds reasonable to me. How about the second thought, "I have the right to tell her what to do when she is living under my roof?" How could you change this thought to achieve your DO of telling Clarise her friend could not come over without upsetting her?

Ty: Well, I could have maybe thought that I have the right to tell Clarise what she needs to do, but if I explain why more specifically, she might be more inclined to listen to me. So, I could tell her that I can't sleep very well when she is up giggling all night, or that I don't want to have to be responsible for someone else's kid.

T: OK, that thought seems like it would lead you to explain more . . . also, I am wondering if this, and the other, remediated thought would decrease your anger rating. What do you think?

Ty: Sure. Yeah, I think so.

T: OK, so your final thought . . . "I can't believe she asked her mother behind my back again!" How could we change it to make it more helpful to getting your DO of telling Clarise her friend could not come over without upsetting her?

Ty: Maybe the thought that I ought to tell Clarise that from now on she needs to get both me and her mom in one room when she wants to ask us for something until she stops trying to play us off of each other.

T: OK, that's kind of a thought and a statement, I guess. Would you be able to have that thought and act on it, do you think? Would that help you to tell Clarise her friend could not come over without upsetting her?

Ty: Well, I'm not sure how much it would impact that, but it probably would help not to make me so angry.

T: Hmmm . . . It sounds like you may have identified a second DO of not getting so angry, huh?

Ty: Yes, I guess so.

T: OK, well, let's finish up with the original DO for now, and we can consider the other one at the next session. How about your behaviors of balling up your fists and talking in a loud tone . . . how could you have changed these behaviors to increase your chances of getting your DO of telling Clarise her friend could not come over without upsetting her?

Ty: Well, I could have made an effort to relax as I spoke to her and could have talked in a normal tone.

T: That sounds like it makes sense.

When you have completed the SA, it might be helpful to discuss with your therapist what you have learned from reviewing the worksheet. You may find that you see common themes or patterns in your interpersonal interactions of which you were not previously aware.

At this point, the SA remediation is complete, as is the SA worksheet. Refer to the form presented in Fig. D.4, on which the most recent changes are in boldface type.

In the case just described, Tyrone expressed a secondary DO in the situation of not getting so angry. This was an admirable and relevant DO, and one likely to be common in anger management therapy. It is a good sign that Tyrone can be objective enough about his behavior to recognize that he wants to get out of the habit of reacting angrily to his children. When dual DOs become evident, as in Tyrone's case, the therapist and client can go through the entire remediation phase twice, looking at each DO separately. Time constraints prohibited this from happening in Tyrone's session, but one of the things he and his therapist might reflect on is that the DO of "not getting so angry" might be one that is common to all of his SAs. In the future, when Tyrone is doing his homework, he may then be more likely to recognize this particular DO immediately and indicate it on his homework sheet.

Another thing to note in this example is that the therapist let Tyrone discover that his initial DO (getting Clarise to obey him without complaint) was not a particularly good one, for reasons indicated in chapter 5. If you do not have an ideal DO, your therapist may choose to point it out to you right away, after some time, or not at all. If your therapist does not point it out to you, you may notice that you are failing to attain your DO, despite having what appear to be "helpful" thoughts and behaviors. If this happens to you, you may want to take a second look at your DO to make sure it is an appropriate one.

Conclusion

Anger is a normal and healthy reaction to some interpersonal situations. However, anger can also be unhealthy if it feels out of control and begins to get you in trouble with important others. If you have noticed that your anger problems have been getting in the way of obtaining what you want in

Tyrone's Second Situational Analysis Worksheet for Anger Management

Name: *Tyrone*

Date of Situational Event: *Monday, April 21, 2004*

Situational Area: ✓ Family ____ Work/School ____ Social

Instructions: Select one stressful event (in which you experienced anger) that has happened to you during the past week and describe it using the format below. Please try to fill out **all** parts of the questionnaire.

---

1. Describe what happened:
Clarise asked if her friend could spend the night with her at our house. I told her "no." She asked me why and I said that there was no need for her friend to sleep over and that what goes on in this family was none of her friend's business. Clarise then went and asked her mother, who told her that her friend could sleep over. When Clarise arrived back at the house with her friend, I sent her friend right out of the house and told Clarise she was grounded for 2 weeks. She told me she hated me and ran upstairs.

2. Describe your interpretation(s) of what happened:
   a. ~~*I can't stand it when that girl doesn't listen to me!*~~ *(Hurtful)* ***Clarise will be more likely to listen to me if I don't overreact and jump down her throat.***
   b. ~~*I have the right to tell her what to do when she is living under my roof.*~~ *(Hurtful)* ***I have the right to tell Clarise what she needs to do, but if I explain why more specifically she might be more inclined to listen.***
   c. ~~*I can't believe she asked her mother behind my back again!*~~ *(Hurtful)* ***I ought to tell Clarise that from now on she needs to get both me and her mom in one room when she wants to ask us for something.***

   2a. List how each of these interpretations made you feel:
   All made me feel angry. On a scale of 1–10 (10 = extreme anger); a. = 9, b. = 7, c. = 9.

3. Describe what you did during the situation:
   a. ~~*Balled up my fists*~~ *(Hurtful)* ***I could have made an effort to relax as I spoke to her***
   b. ~~*Talked in a loud tone*~~ *(Hurtful)* ***I could have talked in a normal tone***

4. Describe how you wanted the event to come out for you (Desired Outcome):
~~*I wanted Clarise to obey me without complaining.*~~ *I wanted to tell Clarise her friend could not come over without upsetting her.*

5. Describe how the event came out for you (Actual Outcome):
Clarise asked her mother behind my back and disobeyed me.

RATE: Was the desired outcome achieved? Yes ____ No ✓

FIG. D.4. Tyrone's Second Situational Analysis Worksheet for Anger Management. Adapted from McCullough (2000) by Bradley A. White, Lorraine R. Reitzel, and Andrea B. Burns.

interpersonal situations, SA can help you to modify your reactions to people so that you increase the chances of getting what you want from others and help prevent alienating others or damaging relationships due to angry outbursts.

CORRECTIONAL ISSUES

If you are reading these materials, it is likely that you are in jail, prison, a detention center, or a forensic hospital. You are probably having some difficulty adjusting to, or coping with, this environment. Perhaps you are having a difficult time getting along with staff or correctional officers, or perhaps the other inmates or patients that you live with have been giving you a hard time. Your difficulty with adjustment may be resulting in multiple disciplinary referrals, majors, or infractions. This may ultimately result in lengthening your commitment sentence or incarceration period. Or, perhaps your difficulty with adjustment is leading to feelings of depression and/or anxiety and has been causing you to feel badly and withdraw from those around you.

You are not alone. Many individuals in correctional environments have difficulty with adjustment and coping. Correctional environments are intentionally different from the "free life" that you previously enjoyed. Whereas you could previously come and go as you'd like, in correctional settings almost all aspects of your life are controlled by staff. This means that when you eat, where you walk, whom you talk to, whom you visit with, what you spend your day doing, and when you sleep is determined by someone other than yourself. This loss of independence and freedom can be quite distressing. As you are aware, correctional environments are not designed to be particularly pleasurable for the people who are sentenced to be there. Difficulty with adjustment and coping in a correctional environment can come out in different ways: Some people may get into a lot of trouble, whereas others may show their pain by keeping to themselves and failing to enjoy the things they once did.

If you find yourself having difficulty coping in a correctional environment, it is important that a trained professional, such as a unit psychologist, psychiatrist, clinical social worker, or medical doctor, evaluate you. This professional will evaluate your symptoms and needs, and recommend a course of treatment that is best suited for your recovery. If you are reading this workbook, it is possible that your treatment professional recommended SA as a part of your treatment.

Incarceration or commitment may make you feel as though you've lost all control over your life. In reality, though, you haven't: There are ways in which you can gain control over what happens to you and influence how things go to increase the chances that you can get what you want in a given situation. Mastery and consistent use of the techniques described in this workbook will help you to feel as if you have control once again over what happens to you. It will start slowly at first, as you begin to apply a new way of thinking and behaving to individual situations. Initially, it may feel foreign and be difficult to get used to. However, eventually you will get the hang of it and begin to see how you can change your thoughts and behaviors to get what you want. Your use of these techniques in a few specific interpersonal situations gradually will begin to generalize to other situations and relationships in your life, and your sense of control and competence will increase. With this increased sense of control, you will begin to feel better, and the behavior that was getting you into trouble with staff and peers should decrease in frequency.

Although you can use this treatment outside of therapy, it works best if you have a therapist who is willing to work with you in reviewing your exercises and helping you with ideas of how to change your thoughts and behaviors. An objective opinion can help to keep you motivated and on track. However, if you faithfully learn and apply these techniques, it is likely that you will not need to be in therapy for long. In fact, the use of SA in therapy was designed to be relatively short term (a few months, rather than a year or more). However, your trained mental health professional (e.g., therapist) is in the best position to make recommendations about treatment duration for your case based on his or her knowledge of you, your symptoms, and your progress in treatment.

Worksheet, Example, and Exercise

The main text of this workbook contains detailed information about how to use SA correctly in the course of your treatment. It provides information about the therapeutic usefulness of each step alone and in conjunction with all of the steps. This part of the Appendix provides a sample worksheet, a case example, and a completed exercise that are specific to adjustment and coping problems frequently encountered in correctional environments.

Sample Worksheet

Let's start with a blank SA worksheet, presented in Fig. D.5, that you can photocopy to use in your work with your therapist. The worksheet is similar to that original SA worksheet, with the exception of a small change to the options of situational areas: They were altered to be more specific to interpersonal interaction in a correctional environment.

Case Example With Completed Exercise

Now that you've had a chance to look at the blank SA worksheet, let's consider a case example that was referred to in chapter 12 of the companion text and is described in further detail here.

George is a 46-year-old, Caucasian male serving his first prison sentence for a sexual offense charge. Prior to his incarceration, he had been employed as a construction site supervisor for almost 20 years. Although he had been arrested and jailed previously for driving under the influence of alcohol and fighting in a bar, he had never received a prison sentence. His current sentence was the result of a plea bargain and was for a minimum of 6 years and a maximum of 10 years. How long he remained in prison was contingent on his behavior during incarceration. George was sent to a medium-custody prison.

George's problems began almost immediately. He felt different from the other inmates, and he believed the staff overlooked him. For example, he saw that other inmates were able to get special treatment (more time outside, trips to the medical bay) if they were loud and argumentative, whereas George's polite requests for special treatment were declined. In addition, other inmates seemed to ignore George (at best) or harass him for cigarettes and candy (at worst). After a few weeks in prison, George put in a self-referral to meet with a member of the mental health staff, because he had been feeling increasingly depressed and was having difficulty sleeping. George was diagnosed with Adjustment Disorder with Depressed Mood. The following is an example from the fourth session of SA:

Therapist (T): OK, George, I see you've brought in your homework for today. Why don't you go ahead and read out loud the situation you've chosen.

Situational Analysis Worksheet Modified for Correctional Settings

Name: ____

Date of Situational Event: ______________________________

Situational Area: ____ Correctional staff ____ Another inmate _____ Other

---

Instructions: Select one stressful event that has happened to you during the past week and describe it using the format below. Please try to fill out **all** parts of the questionnaire.

---

1. Describe what happened:

2. Describe your interpretation(s) of what happened:

3. Describe what you did during the situation:

4. Describe how you wanted the event to come out for you (Desired Outcome):

5. Describe how the event came out for you (Actual Outcome):

RATE: Was the desired outcome achieved? Yes ____ No ____

FIG. D.5. Situational Analysis Worksheet Modified for Correctional Settings. Figure adapted from McCullough (2000) by Lorraine R. Reitzel and Sarah A. Shultz.

George (G): OK. I was standing on line in the chow hall yesterday for lunch, and three guys from my block just cut in front of me in line. I didn't say anything to them at all. Then later I was eating and minding my own business when one of them just walked right up to my plate and took my dessert and walked away. I didn't say anything . . . just finished my food.

T: That's a good example of a situation that we can look at in here. You've described the facts of the situation in a few sentences or less and described it in such a way that I would see it if I were a fly on the wall . . . just observing what actually happened. Tell me your DO.

G: I wanted to stand up for myself.

T: Tell me what "standing up for yourself" would have looked like.

G: Well, I would have said something to them when they cut me in line and when they took my food. Something that would have stopped them from doing it, I guess.

T: OK, so your DO was to stand up for yourself and say something to the guys to stop them from taking advantage of you, right? What was the AO?

G: I got taken advantage of, lost my dessert and ended up spending the rest of my day in my room feeling like crap.

T: Did you achieve your DO in this situation?

G: Uh . . . no.

T: OK, that's important for us to note. Now, tell me what you were thinking during the situation you described.

G: One was I thought I was such a wimp I deserved to be picked on. I also thought that I was pretty stupid for getting myself into prison in the first place to have to deal with all this stuff. Then I thought that from now on I should just skip eating in the chow hall.

T: Those sound like good thoughts to work with. Now behaviors . . . how did you act or what did you say in the situation?

G: Well, I just stood there while they got in front of me, and I guess I looked away from them and tried not to make eye contact. Then I did the same when they took my food.

At this point, all information during the initial step of the SA process has been completed: All five steps of SA have been reviewed and clarified. Figure D.6 is an example of what George's SA worksheet would look like at this point.

The next step of therapy entails the remediation phase of the SA worksheet. As discussed in great detail in this workbook, this phase begins by reviewing the interpretations and behaviors (verbal and nonverbal) as being helpful or hurtful to attaining the specified DO.

T: Now let's look at each thought and behavior and see whether each was helpful or hurtful in reaching your DO of "standing up for yourself." Let's turn our at-

George's Situational Analysis Worksheet for Correctional Settings

Name: *George*

Date of Situational Event: *Monday, April 28, 2004*

Situational Area: ____ Correctional staff _✓_ Another inmate ____ Other

---

Instructions: Select one stressful event that has happened to you during the past week and describe it using the format below. Please try to fill out **all** parts of the questionnaire.

---

1. Describe what happened:
   Okay, I was standing on line in the chow hall yesterday for lunch and three guys from my block just cut in front of me in line. I didn't say anything to them at all. Then later, I was eating and minding my own business when one of them just walked right up to my plate and took my dessert and walked away. I just finished my food.

2. Describe your interpretation(s) of what happened:
   a. *I'm such a wimp I deserved to be picked on.*
   b. *I'm pretty stupid for getting myself into prison in the first place to have to deal with all this stuff.*
   c. *From now on I should just skip eating in the chow hall.*

3. Describe what you did during the situation:
   a. *Stood there*
   b. *Looked away from them*
   c. *Tried not to make eye contact*

4. Describe how you wanted the event to come out for you (Desired Outcome):
   I wanted to say something to them when they cut me in line and when they took my food. Something that would have stopped them.

5. Describe how the event came out for you (Actual Outcome):
   I said nothing, lost my dessert and ended up spending the rest of my day in my room feeling like crap.

RATE: Was the desired outcome achieved? Yes ____ No _✓_

FIG. D.6. George's Situational Analysis Worksheet for Correctional Settings. Figure adapted from McCullough (2000) by Lorraine R. Reitzel and Sarah A. Shultz.

tention to your thoughts now. Take the first interpretation: You thought you were such a wimp you deserved to be picked on. Was that helpful or hurtful in achieving your DO of standing up for yourself?

G: Hurtful. It made me feel weak. It made me feel less like sticking up for myself.

T: OK, how about your second thought about being stupid for getting into prison in the first place. Did that help you or hurt you in achieving your DO of standing up for yourself?

G: It was hurtful. I guess it just distracted me from the issue of being taken advantage of and made me feel weak and stupid.

At this point, George should have written whether his interpretations and behaviors were helpful or hurtful on the SA form. It should look something like the form in Fig. D.7, on which recent changes are in boldface type.

The next step of the remediation phase entails changing the interpretations and behaviors so as to increase the chances of obtaining the DO.

T: OK, so we've established that you had some thoughts and behaviors in this situation that were overall not helpful in getting you to achieve your DO of standing up for yourself. Let's look at them one by one and see if we can change them in some way to heighten the likelihood that they would help you to achieve your DO of standing up for yourself. Let's start with thoughts again. Go ahead.

G: "I'm a wimp and deserved to be picked on." I suppose I could change this to "I'm a human being and deserved to be treated fairly."

T: That sounds good. How does it make you feel?

G: Strong, self-righteous.

T: Would having the thought, "I'm a human being and deserved to be treated fairly" be helpful or hurtful in achieving your DO of standing up for yourself?

G: Helpful. More helpful than my other thought, anyway.

T: OK, how about your next thought?

G: "I'm stupid for getting into prison in the first place" could be changed to, maybe, "I shouldn't have gotten into prison in the first place, but I'm here now and I have to deal with this situation."

T: How does that make you feel?

G: Good and bad, I guess. Maybe more angry at myself than sad, but it also makes me feel like I have to do something to prevent these guys from walking all over me.

T: OK, so would the thought "I shouldn't have gotten into prison in the first place, but I'm here now and I have to deal with this situation" be helpful or hurtful in achieving your DO of standing up for yourself?

G: Definitely helpful.

T: How about the last thought?

George's First Revised Situational Analysis Worksheet for Correctional Settings

Name: *George*

Date of Situational Event: *Monday, April 28, 2004*

Situational Area: ____ Correctional staff ✓ Another inmate ____ Other

---

Instructions: Select one stressful event that has happened to you during the past week and describe it using the format below. Please try to fill out **all** parts of the questionnaire.

---

1. Describe what happened:
   Okay, I was standing on line in the chow hall yesterday for lunch and three guys from my block just cut in front of me in line. I didn't say anything to them at all. Then later I was eating and minding my own business when one of them just walked right up to my plate and took my dessert and walked away. I just finished my food.

2. Describe your interpretation(s) of what happened:
   a. *I'm such a wimp I deserved to be picked on.* ***(Hurtful)***
   b. *I'm pretty stupid for getting myself into prison in the first place to have to deal with all this stuff.* ***(Hurtful)***
   c. *From now on I should just skip eating in the chow hall.* ***(Hurtful)***

3. Describe what you did during the situation:
   a. *Stood there* ***(Hurtful)***
   b. *Looked away from them* ***(Hurtful)***
   c. *Tried not to make eye contact* ***(Hurtful)***

4. Describe how you wanted the event to come out for you (Desired Outcome):
   I wanted to say something to them when they cut me in line and when they took my food. Something that would have stopped them.

5. Describe how the event came out for you (Actual Outcome):
   I said nothing, lost my dessert and ended up spending the rest of my day in my room feeling like crap.

RATE: Was the desired outcome achieved? Yes ____ No ✓

FIG. D.7. George's First Revised Situational Analysis Worksheet for Correctional Settings. Figure adapted from McCullough (2000) by Lorraine R. Reitzel and Sarah A. Shultz.

G: Well, I guess I just shouldn't have had the thought that from now on I could just skip eating in the chow hall. I mean . . . I should be able to eat where everyone else does without problems, right?

T: OK, so does that new thought "I should be able to eat where everyone else does without problems" help you or hurt you in achieving your DO of standing up for yourself?

G: Helps me feel strong and would help me to stand up for myself I think.

T: Well, now that we have the thoughts adjusted, let's move on to changing your behavior to increase the chances of getting your DO of standing up for yourself. Let's take your first behavior of standing there, which you said was hurtful for achieving your DO. How could you change that behavior to increase the chances of getting your DO of standing up for yourself?

G: I could have said something.

T: Like what?

G: Like, "Hey! Sorry," when they cut in line, and then just walked in front of them.

T: Would that have increased the chances of you getting your DO of standing up for yourself?

G: Yes, I think so . . . plus, if I didn't let them cut in front of me I bet they wouldn't have tried to take my dessert, you know?

T: How do you think they would have reacted after you said, "Hey! Sorry," and got in front of them in line?

G: I don't know, I guess they could have just let me, or said something nasty but just let me, or maybe someone would have pushed me out of the way or something.

T: Well, the latter is definitely something to consider. If someone pushed you, what would you have done?

G: I don't know, pushed him back I guess . . . maybe, or maybe done nothing, because it was three against one.

T: Would pushing him back have helped you achieve your DO of standing up for yourself?

G: Yes.

T: So, if you pushed him back, do you think you would have ended up with an infraction and maybe segregation time?

G: Yes, maybe.

T: Is that OK with you?

G: No.

T: Why not?

G: Because I want to make minimum custody at my next evaluation.

T: Oh, so you're saying that you also have a DO of not getting in trouble over this incident?

G: Yeah, I guess so.

T: So, would saying, "Hey! Sorry," and cutting in line in front of the guys have been helpful or hurtful in getting your DO of not getting into trouble?

G: It's hard to say. Maybe it depends on if there are correctional officers nearby . . . if there were, maybe it wouldn't have ended up in a fight.

T: It's a good point. Let's look at your other behaviors . . . what could you have done instead of looking away from them and not making eye contact to get your DO of sticking up for yourself?

G: I could have looked at them and made direct eye contact. That would have probably showed them I had some kind of backbone, you know?

When you have completed the SA, it might be helpful to discuss with your therapist what you have learned from reviewing the worksheet. You may find that you see common themes or patterns in your interpersonal interactions of which you were not previously aware. At this point, the SA remediation stage is complete, as is the SA worksheet. Refer to the form depicted in Fig. D.8, on which the most recent changes are in boldface type.

In George's case, he or the therapist could have made more of the second DO (not getting in trouble over this incident) that was identified during the remediation process. When dual DOs become evident, the therapist and client have the choice of (a) reflecting on both DOs, and choosing the most salient or important one, and using this one to complete the remediation phase of SA, or (b) deciding that both DOs are important and going through the remediation phase with both—that is, the remediation phase would be completed with respect to the first DO and then again with respect to the second DO.

A second DO like the one George had is not uncommon in correctional settings. In fact, this very same second DO of "not getting in trouble" is likely to be a common one for individuals in correctional settings. However, this DO may be more of an afterthought, as primary DOs in correctional settings are usually more immediate, such as getting back at a harassing peer or staff member or pressuring a peer for items of value, such as cigarettes. Remaining out of trouble may seem less salient or important when you are in the heat of a stressful moment. However, one of the values of using SA is in discovering that such secondary goals are important to you and your progress through the correctional system. With practice, you may begin to consider these secondary goals when you are in the midst of stressful situations and thereby modify the way you think and behave in a provocative situation.

George's Second Revised Situational Analysis Worksheet for Correctional Settings

Name: *George*

Date of Situational Event: *Monday, April 28, 2004*

Situational Area: ____ Correctional staff ✓ Another inmate ____ Other

Instructions: Select one stressful event that has happened to you during the past week and describe it using the format below. Please try to fill out *all* parts of the questionnaire.

1. Describe what happened:
   Okay, I was standing on line in the chow hall yesterday for lunch and three guys from my block just cut in front of me in line. I didn't say anything to them at all. Then later I was eating and minding my own business when one of them just walked right up to my plate and took my dessert and walked away. I just finished my food.

2. Describe your interpretation(s) of what happened:
   a. ~~*I'm such a wimp I deserved to be picked on.*~~ *(Hurtful)* ***I'm a human being and deserved to be treated fairly.***
   b. ~~*I'm pretty stupid for getting myself into prison in the first place to have to deal with all this stuff.*~~ *(Hurtful)* ***I shouldn't have gotten into prison in the first place but I'm here now and I have to deal with this situation.***
   c. ~~*From now on I should just skip eating in the chow hall.*~~ *(Hurtful)* ***I should be able to eat where everyone else does without problems.***

3. Describe what you did during the situation:
   a. ~~*Stood there*~~ *(Hurtful)* ***I could have said "Hey! Sorry"***
   b. ~~*Looked away from them*~~ *(Hurtful)* ***I could have looked right at them.***
   c. ~~*Tried not to make eye contact*~~ *(Hurtful)* ***I could have made direct eye contact.***

4. Describe how you wanted the event to come out for you (Desired Outcome):
   I wanted to say something to them when they cut me in line and when they took my food. Something that would have stopped them.

5. Describe how the event came out for you (Actual Outcome):
   I said nothing, lost my dessert and ended up spending the rest of my day in my room feeling like crap.

RATE: Was the desired outcome achieved? Yes ____ No ✓

FIG. D.8. George's Second Revised Situational Analysis Worksheet for Correctional Settings. Figure adapted from McCullough (2000) by Lorraine R. Reitzel and Sarah A. Shultz.

Conclusion

Correctional settings and forensic hospitals are unique and stressful settings that are difficult for most people to adjust to. Adjustment problems in these settings may be quite varied: Some people will act out and get into trouble, some people may find themselves getting anxious or depressed, and some people may find themselves being taken advantage of by others—these are just a few possible outcomes of incarceration. However, if you practice using SA and the techniques described in this book, you will find that your adjustment to this difficult environment will become a little easier. With careful attention to your thoughts, actions, and words, and a focus on your DO in all interpersonal situations, you will soon learn to master your interactions with others and begin to get what you want from situations—even when those situations involve correctional officers or other, more powerful, inmates. Of course, reaching this level of proficiency will take a lot of practice and hard work, and you may find that working with a therapist may be helpful at first, especially if looking at situations in this way is very different from how you usually approach things. However, with practice and perseverance (and maybe some coaching from a therapist!) you will be on your way to getting more control of your life in an environment that was designed to curtail your level of personal control.

References

American Psychiatric Association. (1994). *Diagnostic and statistical manual of mental disorders* (4th ed.). Washington, DC: American Psychiatric Association.

Driscoll, K. A., Cukrowicz, K. C., Reardon, M. L., & Joiner, T. J. (2004). *Simple treatment for complex problems: A flexible approach to psychological difficulties and disorders.* Mahwah, NJ: Lawrence Erlbaum Associates, Inc.

Kaduson, H. G., & Schaeffer, C. E. (2000). *Short-term play therapy for children.* New York: Guilford Press.

McCullough, J. P. (2000). *Treatment for chronic depression: Cognitive behavioral analysis system of psychotherapy.* New York: Guilford Press.

For Product Safety Concerns and Information please contact our
EU representative GPSR@taylorandfrancis.com Taylor & Francis
Verlag GmbH, Kaufingerstraße 24, 80331 München, Germany